EATING OUT
IN GLASGOW

David Phillips

Argyll
publishing

© David Phillips

First published 1993 by
Argyll Publishing
Glendaruel
Argyll PA22 3AE

in association with
Evening Times
195 Albion Street
Glasgow G1 1QP

British Library Cataloguing-in-Publication-Data.
A catalogue record for this book is available from
the British Library.

ISBN 1 874640 45 9

Typeset and electronic output by
Cordfall, Civic Street, Glasgow.
Printed and bound in Great Britain by
HarperCollins, Glasgow.

To
N, P, N and C

Publisher's Note:

All places entered in this guide are commended in some way. They are included in a book which covers the eating out scene in Glasgow because they deserve to be. So while inclusion is a deserved plaudit, it also means that we feel that these establishments are strong enough to bear constructive criticism. We feel sure that critical remarks will be taken in the spirit intended.

The factual information under each review has been supplied by the staff of the eating place. The quoted costs are somewhat arbitrary – they refer to the average cost of a three course meal without drinks.

Closing times generally refer to last orders. Best to check.

While we have tried to ensure that the factual information is accurate, neither author nor publisher can accept responsibility for errors or omissions.

INTRODUCTION

The enormously successful first Evening Times Guide to Eating Out in Glasgow was published in 1990 to coincide with Glasgow's reign as European City of Culture. It reported on the increase in the number of eating places in recent years and the vast range of the food now on offer.

Even one generation ago, eating out was not as popular as it now is. Scottish high teas in hotel dining rooms and sedate afternoon tea in a very few tearooms and restaurants were the limited experience of many. Asking for food in a pub would have marked you out as a foreigner.

Now things are very different. Glaswegians going on far-flung holidays have brought back higher expectations on range and quality. The experience of eating as a pleasure has also been imported to Scottish culture. The arrival of the various immigrant groups over the years has challenged local cuisine, pushing tastes wider and standards higher. The influx of the fast food chains, which has continued apace since 1990, has also led the populace to expect to eat out as a matter of course.

So eating out in Glasgow continues to thrive. Surveying the restaurant scene as we approach 1994, it would be unrealistic to ignore the effects of the economic recession. Some famous gourmet temples have disappeared since the last Guide, such as the relatively short-lived October in Bearsden or the much-lamented Colonial in the High Street. Other old favourites, such as the once peerless Rogano, have held grimly on but are perhaps not what they once were.

As a result of all the changes, the time is ripe for this new Eating Out in Glasgow. All visits have been anonymous and not one free lunch has been accepted. Opinions are mine based on visits to the establishments listed. You, the reader, may arrive at different conclusions.

Regrettably it has not been possible to sample and enter the many good out-of-town eating places. If your favourite eating place has been excluded, don't take offence – write and let me know.

The philosophy underlying all the comments made is that eating out should be an enjoyable all round experience. An important (but not the sole) criterion is the food quality. Others include the setting, service, atmosphere and price. Those wanting a gourmet's guide should look elsewhere.

Most of the gripes aired in the first edition bear repetition. Glasgow still lacks, unaccountably, a major rallying point for the growing army of vegetarians. Smoking policies remain perplexingly tolerant of the smokers – unlike other cities and other countries, it's the non-smokers who appear to be discriminated against. And in innumerable delis, cafes and sandwich bars, "the personal touch" with hands on food means that hygiene falls down. Why not wear gloves or use tongs?

Facilities for the disabled are steadily improving but many establishments have a long way to go – one had gone to the effort of fitting disabled toilet facilities but there was no wheelchair access! Furniture and fittings in some places are in need of attention. And live music in eating places remains rare.

On the positive side, restaurants and other places serving food continue to proliferate. The cafe-bar, as epitomised by the Gandolfi or Baby Grand, is more widespread in Glasgow than in any other major British city. Children are at last receiving recognition as a welcome group with special needs. Food portions are becoming ever more substantial in deference to the rising expectations of those numerous Glaswegians who have experienced American generosity at first hand. Thankfully, the transient aberration of La Nouvelle Cuisine is fast receding into the mists of time.

Crystal ball gazing is always hazardous, but the outlook seems promising for Glasgow food lovers providing that we all keep a watchful eye on standards. This book offers a modest contribution to the cause.

Happy eating!

David Phillips,
September 1993

THE WEST END

The West End is usually regarded as the most attractive part of central Glasgow, dominated as it is by the impressive Gilbert Scott Building of Glasgow University overlooking Kelvingrove Park. The main thoroughfare is Byres Road which runs from stately Great Western Road at the top end down to bustling Partick Cross at the bottom. Apart from the University, with its fine Hunterian Museum and Gallery, other highlights of the area include the Kelvingrove Art Gallery and Museum and the Museum of Transport. To the north and west are the prosperous suburbs of Bearsden and Milngavie.

AMBER
130 Byres Road, G12   339 6121/8970

The consistency of this well-liked Cantonese restaurant over many years is remarkable. If you can avoid the cluster of ill-placed tables in the centre of the room, the comfort score is high. Another major plus is the immaculate cleanliness – table cloths are changed after every use.

The menu goes on for ever; even the business lunch has 9 European and 40 Chinese options! Chicken noodle soup was near-perfect – unfortunately served without bread. Beef szechuan made a vigorous impression and was plentiful. Anything tastes good in their sweet and sour sauce. Seafood is a special interest of the kitchen and wins compliments. The desserts are under a pound a time.

A transiently encouraging sign was the presence of a group of oriental customers who seemed perfectly happy with the proceedings; on closer inspection, it transpired that they were tucking into what looked like haddock and chips with great relish.

A restful sort of place where the unfussy staff allow you to sip your Chinese tea in slow motion.

Main food style: Chinese/Cantonese/Pekingese
Licensed: Yes
Tables: Smoking 17; Non–smoking 1
Approximate cost: £10 – £22
Cards: Access; AmEx; Diners; Visa
Open: M–F 12.00–14.00, 17.00–23.30; Sat 15.00–24.00;
       Sun 17.00–23.30
Disabled access: Yes

ASHOKA WEST END
1284 Argyle Street, G3   339 0936/3371

The Ashoka started out from modest beginnings but the name is known all over the city (and probably beyond). Curiously, the source of this popularity is not immediately apparent. The restaurant has always provided plain, unsophisticated Indian dishes to a large and steadfast clientele at moderate prices. There is nothing flamboyant either about the food or its presentation. And the restaurant itself is an unsympathetic place with no hallway; every time the door opens, all heads turn in unison to inspect the newest arrivals.

The Punjabi menu is notable for lamb, chicken and thali variations. Flavours are subdued, spices are not too fiery. Portions are adequate.

Consistency rather than brilliance is the hallmark of the kitchen. Despite the lack of frills (or maybe because of them), mobs of ravenous youngsters descend on the place late on a Friday and Saturday night. For some reason, the management seem determined not to open at lunchtime.

Main food style: Indian
Licensed: Yes
Tables: Smoking 20; Non–smoking 0
Approximate cost: £8 – £14
Cards: All major cards
Open: M–Sun 17.00–00.30
Disabled access: None

ASHOKA
19 Ashton Lane, G12   357 5904

Once the site of a Chinese restaurant, the Ashoka seemed to get off to a slow start. Now it is one of the most popular Indian restaurants in the city. The seating has been redesigned and the room is almost unrecognisable. In the evening, a vast mural occupying an entire wall is illuminated to spectacular effect.

The menu is full of surprises: machi massala is made with spicy cod; chicken or lamb served Goanese fashion, with creamed coconut sauce along with yoghurt, fresh cream and green chillies; nawabi dishes, in which the meat is simmered in a Karahi until lightly cooked and then added to a base of fried onion, fried mushroom, capsicum and tomato. These are all about £7.

Vegetarians are happy – they have their own changing blackboard menu of curries, although they have many other options. A la carte prices are fairly high, but there are budget priced lunches and a set meal for two at £19.95 or for four at £34.95. In the evening, parking is a lot easier than during the day. Worth a visit – even if only to see the mural!

Main food style: Indian
Licensed: Yes
Tables: Smoking 20; Non–smoking 0
Approximate cost: £3.95 – £11
Cards: All major cards
Open: M–T 12.00–24.00; F&Sat 12.00–00.30;
      Sun 17.00–24.00
Disabled access: Yes

BACK ALLEY
8 Ruthven Lane, G12   334 7165

There's an idiosyncratic, lively feel to this outfit which compensates for its den-like dimensions and at times cacophonous background music.

The menu veers to Southern US and burgers are much in evidence, but the blackboard may appeal more. There is a curious tendency to exclude soup (excellent) from the cheapie lunch menu. Potato skins work well, as do lasagna and your common-or-garden fish and chips. No problem for vegetarians. Some of the ethnic exotica are heavily spiced. House wine is good value, but the white (as so often happens) is aimed at the sweet-toothed. Service is efficient, cheerful. Average age of the diners seems youthful. Have a wander down the lane to find the competition (PJ's, Di Maggio's) as well as some of the strangest shops in the city.

Main food style: American
Licensed: Yes
Tables: Smoking 19, Non-smoking 0
Approximate cost: £5 – £12
Cards: Access; AmEx; Eurocard; Mastercard; Visa;
        Young Scot Card
Open: M–F 12.00–15.00; M–T 17.00–23.00;
        F 17.00–24.00; Sat 12.00–23.00;
        Sun 12.30–24.00
Disabled access: Yes

BALBIR's ASHOKA TANDOORI
108 Elderslie Street, G3   221 1761

This was the original Balbir's before he expanded up
the road to the Vegetarian Ashoka and the Indian
Brasserie. At one time, the cogniscenti regarded it as
the finest Indian restaurant in Glasgow (and therefore
the world).

While still commanding a large following, there are
rivals who might have a stronger claim to the
championship title nowadays. Packed to the gunnells
on weekend evenings, you can have real trouble
getting a table – booking in advance seemed only to
confer a slight advantage. The crowds are drawn by
the no-nonsense, value-for-money approach. The
cooking is reasonably consistent and occasionally
inspired. Portions are generous and the strength of
the spices can be adjusted to suit your taste. Try beef
shahi bahar (a korma prepared with ground nuts and
cream with almond flakes) or chicken tikka komal
patia (a less pungent version of the normal patia). If
you feel like going berserk, you can feast on leg of
lamb shahi massalum for a mere £44.95 for four – but
you should give the kitchen 24 hours notice.
(Presumably they feed you poppadoms while you're
waiting.) There's an ultra-cheap business lunch
(£3.25) and a pre-theatre (£6.50) which is served at
complicated times.

Main food style: Indian
Licensed: Yes
Tables: Smoking 39; Non–smoking 6
Approximate cost: £7.50 – £15
Cards: All major cards
Open: M–T 12.00–23.30; F&Sat 12.00–00.30,
        Sun 17.00–23.30
Disabled access: No

BALBIR's VEGETARIAN ASHOKA
141 Elderslie Street, G3   248 4407

Vegetarians can find adequate sustenance in most half-decent Indian restaurants, but some adhere to the discipline of avoiding meat or fish produce entirely, even if it's only being consumed at the next table. This one is as strict as they come and in consequence has its own select fan club.

Interestingly, even the most unashamed carnivores have been known to opt for a vege-curry once in a blue moon – and have thoroughly enjoyed it. The other great attraction is economic: you can eat your way through the most gargantuan portions of vegetable masalas, stuffed parathas and vegetarian thalis and still end up having to fork out astonishingly little cash.

In its earlier years, reports were ecstatic from some quarters. Nowadays approval is more muted but that may simply reflect the loss of novelty value. Incidentally, the view of Park Towers from Elderslie Street is glorious.

Main food style: Indian/Vegetarian
Licensed: Yes
Tables: Smoking 13; Non-smoking 0
Approximate cost: £6 – £12
Cards: All major cards
Open: 7 days 17.00–23.30
Disabled access: Yes, but toilets downstairs

La BAVARDE
19 New Kirk Road, G61   942 2202

As might be expected from its name, La Bavarde has attracted the chattering classes from Bearsden and beyond for many years. A major factor in its appeal is that the regular clientele know exactly what to expect week in week out – long-term reliability is a precious commodity in the dining scene.

The room is attractively furnished and comfortable. The evening menu is almost illegible but repays careful attention as you munch on a slice of sensational aniseed flavoured bread. Starters (£2 – £3) include paw paw with stilton, vegetarian red lentil pate and squid veronique. Celery and parsnip soup was wonderful, chicken liver pate was smooth and light. Roast duck was crispy without being overdone. Other accomplished main courses were veal and chardonnay pie (with a sharpish tang which may not always please) and brill and ginger en croute, a risky creation realised with flair. Desserts were not quite in the same class, but coffee comes with tablet and refills are offered. The staff displayed such an eagerness that might not always be conducive to a relaxed atmosphere.

Main food style: French/European
Licensed: Yes
Tables: Smoking 18; Non–smoking 0
Approximate cost: £7 – £20
Cards: Access; AmEx; Diners; Visa
Open: T–Sat 12.00–13.30, 18.30–21.30; Sun&M Closed
Disabled access: Yes

The BAY TREE
403 Great Western Road, G4   334 5898

Vegetarians are often the butt of music hall jokes, but they should be taken seriously by the catering and restaurant trade. Their numbers are growing, particularly in the younger age groups, and they can already exert a degree of consumer clout. Unfortunately, Glasgow has let its vegetarian citizens down badly over the years.

The Bay Tree is one of the very few attempts to meet their needs. It's a superficially wacky and chaotic place, tending perhaps to reinforce those comic stereotypes, but it merits a closer look. There's no menu as such, with frequently changing dishes of the day (such as curries and pastas) displayed on blackboards. Pea and mint soup (£1) is thick and creamy with a pleasant tangy flavour. Baked potatoes are generously filled. Salads are fresh and attractive: a large one (£3) is ample for a meal. Hot drinks are excellent, and you can drink decaffeinated coffee. One small customer was devastated to discover that no Coke is stocked – is that on principle? The premises are on the cramped side and furniture is far from ideal. But the food is tasty and inexpensive and there is no shortage of customers. We need competitors, please. . .

Main food style: Vegetarian & Vegan
Licensed: No
Tables: Smoking 3; Non–smoking 6
Approximate cost: £5 – £6
Cards: None
Open: T–F 11.00–21.00; Sat 10.00–21.00;
          Sun 11.00–20.00; M closed
Disabled access: Yes

BONHAM's
194 Byres Road, G12   357 3424

When one considers the potential, Byres Road is
something of a disappointment in terms of its pub-
eateries. Bonham's is a standard-setter (where are the
others?) in creating a Chelsea-style wine bar with
appetising hot and cold snacks served either with
alcohol or coffee.

The menu is undeniably short, but the soups,
croissants, salads and quiches are reliable, tasty and
reasonably priced. The seating is plush, the decor
different: the building is said once to have been a
cinema lobby. Don't miss the superb naturally lit
stained glass window on the first floor. Staff are
pleasant and believed (by themselves) to be the most
intelligent and attractive in the West End. Would
probably go unnoticed on the Fulham Road, but for
the West of Scotland, Bonham's is a small miracle.

Main food style: British
Licensed: Yes
Tables: Smoking 16; Non–smoking 0
Approximate cost: £3 – £8
Cards: Access; Visa
Open: M–T 10.00–23.00; F&Sat 10.00–24.00;
         Sun 12.00–23.00
Disabled access: No

The CABIN
996-998 Dumbarton Road, G14   954 7102

Every now and then, a major new cooking talent
bursts on the scene. Sooner or later that talent is
recognised, cultivated and marketed to the point
where the prices of the product soar out of reach of
the ordinary mortal. The chef of The Cabin is such a
talent, as yet thankfully "undiscovered", and offering
meals of supreme quality at normal prices to a
delighted and rapidly growing public.

The exterior is unpromising, the dining room is
nothing special – but the food is extraordinary. For
£18, you get three courses and coffee. Carrot and
orange soup will get you off to a quiet but satisfying
start. Thereafter, choose lamb stuffed with haggis,
salmon en croute, seafood – anything – and enjoy.
It's all terrific. Vegetables are glorious: red cabbbage,
ratatouille and potatoes dauphinois making a
welcome change from carrots and beans. Of the
desserts, caramel and walnut mousse or bread and
butter pudding will do nicely. Although licensed, you
can BYOB for £1 corkage. The Cabin is one of a kind
– and it may prove hard going to sustain these
remarkably high standards. Meanwhile, Whiteinch
can boast of having one of the best restaurants in
Scotland. Highly recommended.

Main food style: International
Licensed: Yes
Tables: Smoking 16; Non–smoking 0
Approximate cost: £18 for 4 course set menu
Cards: None
Open: T–Sun 12.30–14.00, Dinner from 19.30
Disabled access: Yes

CAFE de COURCY
5 Cresswell Lane, G12   334 6776

This lane never fully recovered from the closure of
Ashby's auction house some years ago, but the De
Courcy arcade has managed to survive along with its
popular cafe. The predictable menu seldom changes
and that may be an attraction for the regulars.
Presumably, the low prices play their part.

Baked potatoes and toasties come well garnished
(discounting the unappetising cole-slaw) and the
service is invariably brisk and friendly. The once
outstanding omelettes are now merely very good,
and the chips remain the right colour, texture and
taste. The baking is worth a second look. Coffee
(especially cappuccino) could be better.

Hygiene seems top-notch but is too-frequently
spoiled by the billowing clouds of cigarette smoke
when the chain-smoking brigade arrive. Commands
affection despite its faults.

Main food style: British
Licensed: No
Tables: Smoking 13; Non–smoking 1
Approximate cost: £5 – £8
Cards: None
Open: M–Sat 9.00–17.00; Sun 12.00–17.00
Disabled access: Yes

CAFE JJ

180 Dumbarton Road, G11　　　357 1881

"How Green is My Cafe" could be the theme song of the manager of JJ. Tablecloths, curtains, staff T-shirts – all are meticulously colour-matched to pleasing effect. This is one of the most bustling cafes in the West End. Everything about the place carries the stamp of quality, from the cleverly constructed menu to the smartly attired servers.

As well as trad cafe fare, there are numerous more adventurous touches: peat-smoked haddock (unmissable), wholemeal pizza, chicken a la king. Baking highlights among the blackboard specials – strawberry pavlova (could have been better, but it's a difficult one to bring off), tropical fruit torte. All the hot drinks are worth a try with tea a bargain at 60p a pot.

Seating (padded) is unusually comfortable, and the lace curtain prevents the unwelcome attentions of passing pedestrians. If you are on wheels, beware of deadly traffic wardens on the prowl on Dumbarton Road.

Main food type: British/ International
Licensed: Yes
Tables: Smoking 7; Non–smoking 3
Approximate cost: £6 – £10
Cards: None
Open: M–W 10.30–19.30; T–Sat 10.30–21.30;
　　　Sun 12.00–18.00
Disabled access: No

Il CAPPUCCINO
18a Gibson Street, G12   339 7195

A magnet to the academic fraternity, the takeaway
counter serves the best sandwiches in the area
(though even the regular customers must wish the
staff would wear gloves when handling food).
Superb range of deli dishes: soups, pastas, bagels,
pastrami, salads – you get the picture. A personal
favourite – hot croissant with cambazola. Good
baking and coffee. Quantities are not vast. Tranquil
staff despite the lunch rush.

Downstairs (windowless) has a different ambience
and has the budget business lunch which starts well
with home-made soup, continues satisfactorily with a
modest choice of reliable main courses but then
seems to peter out with disappointing desserts. Minor
grumbles apart, people keep coming back.

Main food style: Italian/European
Licensed: Yes
Tables: Smoking 15; Non–smoking 0
Approximate cost: £4 – £10
Cards: Access; Visa
Open: M–F 11.45–14.30, 17.00–22.00; Sat 11.45–22.45;
**   Sun 11.45–21.00**
Disabled access: No

COTTIERS
93-95 Hyndland Street, G11   357 5825

One of the perennial problems facing any urban planner is deciding what to do about crumbling but architecturally meritorious old buildings. Glasgow entrepreneurs have come up with a highly effective answer – turn them into restaurants.

In this case, the A-listed Dowanhill Parish Church, strategically straddling the borders of Partick, Hyndland and Dowanhill, has been saved from oblivion by an ambitious scheme to convert it into a multi-purpose cultural centre. The exterior is covered in grime but is clearly a fine example of the work of Leiper who collaborated on this project with an interior designer by the name of – wait for it – Cottier. The theatre (in the main section of the church) is not yet complete at the time of writing.

Meanwhile, a functional bar with some very basic outside tables (could not decent seats and pretty umbrellas have been found for this courtyard?) is functioning. This serves a three course lunch (around £6) prepared by the kitchen of the main rooftop restaurant which specialises in Mexican dishes (nachos, enchiladas, tortillas and more) at higher prices. Early reports of the cooking and presentation are enthusiastic – whether consistency will be maintained remains to be seen. Worth a detour for.

Main food style: Mexican
Licensed: Yes
Tables: Smoking 30; Non-smoking 0
Approximate cost: £12 – £18
Cards: All except AmEx
Open: Sun–T 17.00–22.30; F&S 17.00–00.30
Disabled access: Only in bar

CREME de la CREME
1071 Argyle Street, G2   221 3222

Many Glaswegians will recall, with mixed degrees of nostalgia, the cinema, concert hall and bingo parlour which were the successive previous functions of this externally unappealing building. Never in its history has looked as it does now, an extravagant temple of Indo-Glasgow eating. The interior design is quite stunning in style, scale and colour. There are waterfalls, sculptures, gleaming chrome fittings and plush carpets. With all of this on which to feast the eye, who needs food? Should you decide to eat, head straight for the balcony buffet which is a novel experience for those unaquainted with it.

Select your starter and main courses from the bemusing expanse of hot plates beckoning you to try out any and every combination. Downstairs is the more conventional (and expensive) a la carte format. The food is copious and tasty on both levels. Unusually for an Indian establishment, much attention has been paid to the preparation of the desserts which are superb. Droves of uniformed waiters attend to your every whim. Certainly a new and highly theatrical dimension to Indian eating in Glasgow. In the lobby of the ground floor section there is an amazing spherical water-sculpture – how on earth does it work?

Main food style: Indian
Licensed: Yes
Tables: Smoking 25; Non–smoking 75
Approximate cost: £8 – £16
Cards: All major cards
Open: M–Sat 12.00–24.00; Sun 17.00–24.00
Disabled access: Yes

CUL-de-SAC

44 Ashton Lane, G12   334 1284

Ashton Lane once housed the servants and stables of the gentry living up the hill in Lilybank Gardens. These days, it has become a kind of mini-Hampstead with its cinema, pubs and restaurants lining a narrow cobbled street.

The Cul-de-Sac, at the far end, is in two parts: a lively upstairs pub which does excellent bar lunches, and an unusual restaurant on the ground floor specialising in crepes (watch how you pronounce it). The menu is an interesting cultural Franco-Scottish hybrid but the crepes should be the focus of your meal. They are superb – the chef times them to perfection and doesn't skimp on the fillings. Side dishes and desserts are similar in scale and quality. Only Sumo wrestlers may feel peckish after three courses. Wine by the glass is expensive. Coffee is above average. Thankfully a business lunch has been introduced.

Not the most physically comfortable place for protracted conversation or quiet contemplation, but has improved over the years.

Main food style: British/French
Licensed: Yes
Tables: Smoking 23; Non–smoking 0
Approximate cost: £12 – £20
Cards: Access; AmEx; Mastercard; Visa
Open: Sun–T 12.00–23.00; F&Sat 12.00–24.00
Disabled access: Yes

One DEVONSHIRE GARDENS
1 Devonshire Gardens, G12   334 9494

Sceptics pronounced ODG dead on arrival – too upmarket for Glasgow, they claimed. They were wrong. The hotel has now expanded along the terrace and the restaurant is as absurdly luxurious as ever. The drawing room where you have your pre-prandial sherry is an awesome sight, with its vast drapes and period fireplace. The dark colours and effusive service induce an atmosphere of almost stifling formality – notice how the guests all converse in an undertone.

Prices are about as high as you'll encounter anywhere in the city. Even afternoon tea is £9 a head. Lunch is £19 and the dinner (four courses) is a whopping £35. This latter is a grand procession of seafood and game delicacies, with the exception of the consomme. Star turns include the fillet of sea bass with basil and fennel sauce on a bed of pesto noodles, braised guinea fowl with a wild mushroom and tarragon sauce, and sauteed cannon of lamb with a truffle and olive potato. The desserts are chosen from a separate menu. The wine list is designed to help you haemorrhage more money. Is it worth it? If you have the luck – and the means – to wish to celebrate with full pomp and circumstance, you might as well do it here.

Main food style: British
Licensed: Yes
Tables: 12; Non–smoking catered for
Approximate cost: £19 – £35
Cards: All major cards
Open: Sun–F 12.00–14.00, 19.00–22.30;
          Sat 19.00–22.30
Disabled access: Yes

GINGER HILL
1 Hillhead Street, G62   956 6515

The village of Milngavie is more than a far-flung
dormitory suburb of the big city. If you know where
to look, you'll come across hidden treasures known
only to a select few. Ginger Hill is one of them.
There is little point in attempting to explain how to
reach it – just seek and ye shall find.

The dining room is small but not oppressive, with a
partition which breaks up the floor space. The menu
is brief and specialises in fish, shellfish and vegetarian
dishes. The quality of the cooking is so remarkable
that anything you choose will be memorable. Starters
are imaginatively constructed and the soups are in a
class of their own. Of the fish dishes, red snapper,
sole, monkfish and squid are recurring items – they
are all supremely well cooked and presented with
appropriate garnishings and vegetables. Desserts are
similarly superlative and should on no account be
missed. The staff recognise the importance of
matching the skills of the kitchen to the individual
requirements of the diner. Although the evening
dinner prices are high (as opposed to the lunch
menu from which you can select light, inexpensive
snacks), you will receive in return a meal which you
will recall with pleasure for many months. That is
value for money. Highly recommended.

Main food style: Scottish/French
Licensed: No, BYOB (No Corkage Charge)
Tables: Smoking 7; Non-smoking 0
Approximate cost: £10 – £25
Cards: Access; AmEx; Diners; Visa
Open: M–Sat 11.00–16.00,
      Dinner 19.00–'till late (One sitting only)
Disabled access: No

GROSVENOR CAFE
31-35 Ashton Lane, G12   339 1848

Never-change-a winning-formula has been the motto
of the Grosvenor for what seems like about a
century. Not so much a cafe as a way of life, tables
are as hard to come by as ever particularly in
university term time. If you look closely at the menu,
there have been innovations to the point where you
can work your way through a substantial 3-course
meal and still avoid a double-figure bill.

The set lunch is even cheaper (under £5). Soup
remains tasty and nourishing, and vegeburgers in
various guises are in great demand. For that mid-
morning "little something" so beloved of Peruvian
bears and others, a hot croissant with butter and a
small pot of strawberry jam is sufficiently pleasing to
compensate for the underpowered coffee. Won't win
prizes for presentation (are chipped tea plates really
necessary?) or ventilation, but cannot be ignored. No
corkage charge if you BYOB.

Main food style: European
Licensed: No
Tables: Smoking 10; Non-smoking 2
Approximate cost: £4 – £6
Cards: None
Open: M–Sat 9.00–23.00; Sun 11.00–18.00
Disabled access: Yes

JANSSEN's

1355 Argyle Street, G3   334 9682

The huge number of visitors attracted to Kelvingrove and the Kelvin Hall presumably have to eat somewhere, sometime, and the local options available to them are scandalously limited. Janssen's must pick up a high proportion of this trade and deservedly so. The harsh interior design is not exactly user-friendly but the consistently high standard of the food is the decisive factor.

Menu changes have been few over the years with the exception of the blackboard specials which at their best can be outstanding. Soups and starters are especially effective. Vegetable satay has many devotees, hummus generates more criticism. Portions, including those of garnishings and side dishes, are as they should be. Desserts are erratic, coffee is superb. True to the loosely Northern European origins of the place, the staff could hardly be accused of excessive levity.

Main food style: International
Licensed: Yes
Tables: Smoking 12; Non–smoking 0
Approximate cost: £6 – £12
Cards: Access; Eurocard; Mastercard; Visa
Open: M–T 12.00–22.30; F&Sat 12.00–23.00;
          Sun 12.00–21.00
Disabled access: Yes

The JEELIE PIECE
517a Great Western Road, G12   337 1852

The inspired name of this microscopic cafe causes heads to turn on Great Western Road. There are about six tables which fill up rapidly at lunchtime. The menu is displayed on three blackboards which can induce a nasty crick in your neck if you have trouble making up your mind. The decor is idiosyncratic – like a Scottish baronial hall in miniature with wooden beams, tartan drapes and a cut-out horse where you expect the moose. The staff are welcoming and must love dealing with the public – they could scarcely get much closer to them.

You can eat all day from breakfast through to an evening meal. The set afternoon tea looks inviting. There's no set lunch but a wide choice of garnished croissants, bagels, baguettes or baked potatoes. Brown or white bread is available. Fillings are imaginative: eggs and tarragon, French tomato with basil, hummus, roast beef and cranberry sauce, spicy shrimp, scrambled egg and onion (around £3). Hot dishes include tuna pasta, chicken satay with rice (about £4).

One problem which will have to be addressed is what to do about smokers. In a place this size, a complete ban should be imposed – business would only benefit.

Main food style: Scottish
Licensed: No
Tables: Smoking 6; Non-smoking 0
Approximate cost: £5 – £15
Cards: Access; Visa
Open: M-S 10.00–22.00; Sun 12.00–17.00
Disabled access: Yes, but no disabled toilet

JOE's GARAGE
52 Bank Street, G12   339 5407

Few could have predicted that an outfit as zany as
this would survive – indeed thrive – for so long. The
magic formula is a combination of rock-bottom prices
and enjoyable food. The set lunch (£1.95 for two
courses and coffee) has held its startlingly low price-
tag for as long as most of the people can remember.
Students are the obvious market but all age groups
appreciate a genuine bargain.

The room itself defies description – the famous petrol
pump is still there. Tables are perhaps too close
together for comfort and the music can be intrusive.
The menu has become less Mexican-oriented than in
the past. Vegetable soup would have been OK had it
been hotter. Lasagne was terrific, fish and chips were
mediocre. Numerous beers to choose from. Lunch
portions are (unsurprisingly) more modest than the
evening equivalents.

Vegetarians please note: as well as plenty of choices
on the standard menu, you can have non-meat
"sausages" in your full British breakfast. Service is
invariably faultless.

Main food type: Italian
Licensed: Yes
Tables: Smoking 17; Non–smoking 0
Approximate cost: £3 – £8.75
Cards: Access; AmEx; Visa
Open: M–F 12.00–15.00, 17.00–24.00; Sat 12.00–24.00;
      Sun 11.00–24.00
Disabled access: No

KILLERMONT POLO CLUB
2022 Maryhill Road, G20   946 5412

The old Killermont House was a traditional Franco-Scottish restaurant which used to ttracted a large following. When the Polo Club took over, there were mutterings of doubt whether this part of the city could retain high quality eateries. And did Glasgow need yet another Indian restaurant? The Polo Club has given its potential critics a strong affirmative answer. Some say this is now the best of its type in the city. The building itself is as elegant as ever, overlooking what looks at first to be an ordinary garden. In fact, it's a miniature polo field complete with pavilion and crest!

The lunch menu offers a choice of 8 starters (such as vegetable pakora, mushroom purri, salad of chicken tikka and orange with corriander vinegrette) and about 15 main courses including tikkas, kormas and patias. There are always vegetable dishes. Two courses are £6.95, three courses £7.95. In the evening, you can have dishes such as spiced lentil cakes in yoghurt medley (£1.95), parsi fish parcels which comprise plaice fillets wrapped in spinach, served with a Karahi sauce and lemon rice (£7.50), or any from a range of traditional tandoori and other classics. The cooking and presentation are assured throughout. This is Indian dining (Scottish style) at its most sophisticated.

Main food style: Indian
Licensed: Yes
Tables: Smoking 25; Non–smoking 0
Approximate cost: £8 – £20
Cards: All major cards
Open: M–F 12.00–14.00, 17.00–23.00;
       Sat&Sun 17.00–23.00
Disabled access: Yes

The LIVING ROOM
5-9 Byres Road, G11   339 8511

Brazilian restaurants are not exactly ten-a-penny in this part of the world so this new venture should arouse curiosity if nothing else. It's an enigmatic little place with an austerity of decor that presumably expresses an uncompromising aesthetic philosophy (in Portuguese?). The chairs have been likened to coat hangers – those who have tried them admit some surprise at the experience.

The food is spicy but highly palatable: franco a passarino (marinated chicken pieces deep-fried in olive oil and garlic served with tzatziki and salad) is typical. A more exotic dish is moqueca de piexe (casserole of fish, prawns and peppers cooked in coconut milk, palm oil and chilli pepper served with rice and salad). Have some liquid refreshment handy to wash these down.

Whether any of the cooking is as authentic as it sounds is difficult for the novice to judge. But if the locals like it, The Living Room will enjoy a long and prosperous future. One to watch.

Main food styles: Brazilian/Vegetarian
Licensed: Yes
Tables: Smoking 18; Non-smoking 0
Approximate cost: £4 – £8
Cards: All major cards
Open: 7 days 12.00–19.30 (last orders)
Disabled access: Yes

Di MAGGIO's (West End)
61 Ruthven Lane, G12   334 8560

Immensely popular if arguably least attractive branch
of the Di Maggio network, the colour red is the
theme here throughout – on carpet, curtains,
tablecloths, light fittings. Fine Hollywood nostalgia
photography (including Marilyn, of course) adorns
the walls. There's even a platform at one end
enhancing the showbiz impression. Seating is
ludicrously cramped in the centre of the room. An
awkward step near the kitchen repeatedly caused the
waitress to trip.

Fairly extensive menu majors in pizzas and pastas.
Lentil soup was an unhappy choice (oversalted), the
minestrone fine. Pizzas are state-of-the-art with bases
neither too heavy nor too thin, which explains the
brisk trade in takeaways. Pastas are also top class,
and the main dishes come decently garnished. Ice
cream is in the best Italian tradition. Children love the
place so families are often in evidence. Reliable,
clean and good value if unexciting. Shame about the
lay-out.

Main food style: Italian
Licensed: Yes
Tables: Smoking 27, Non–smoking 0
Approximate cost: £5 – £15
Cards: All except Diners
Open: M–F 12.00–14.30, 17.00–24.00; Sat 12.00–01.00;
          Sun 17.00–24.00
Disabled access: No

The MARINER
351 Dumbarton Road, G11   357 0206

Dumbarton Road has always been a lively shopping street replete with pubs but has never really attracted restaurants or cafes in any numbers. A slow improvement is taking place and this new coffee house is leading the way.

The decor is modernistic and plain, almost to the point of harshness. The wide glass frontage creates a goldfish bowl effect. These are minor quibbles. The Mariner is clean, efficient and friendly. The menu is geared to snacks and these are invariably fresh, attractively garnished and tasty. What starts out as a simple baked potato comes on a tray with a substantial side-salad. Coffee and cake mid-morning or afternoon is probably more enjoyable than lunch if you want a quiet corner table. Once again, quality breeds success – even in deepest Partick.

Main food style: British
Licensed: No
Tables: Smoking 11; Non-smoking 0
Approximate cost: £6 – £10
Cards: None
Open: M–W 09.30–17.30; T 09.30–19.00;
**   F&S 09.30–18.00; Sun 12.00–17.00**
Disabled access: Yes

MATA HARI

17 West Princes Street, G4   332 9789

This little gem of a restaurant does not deserve its present location at the end of a one way street off St George's Road (not exactly the Champs Elysee of the North). Those who can read maps will receive a warm reception and a delightful meal. The discouraging iron gate leads down some steps into a comfortable den of a room.

The menu uses Malay terms to describe the food but there is an adequate English translation. Rice, vegetables and spices are recurring ingredients. The business lunch (about £6) is good value, but the set evening dinner (£17.50) is something of an oriental feast. Among the most intriguing dishes are acar (mixed vegetable pickle with sesame seeds in spiced lemon grass sauce) and ikan halia (fish cooked with shredded ginger, chilli and soya bean sauce). Soto ayam (mixed vegetable soup) was delicious, as was kari ayam (chicken with potato and coconut cream). Portions are generous. Service is charming. Glaswegians may be wary of Eastern cooking which is neither Indian nor Cantonese, but thankfully enough of them are giving this one the benefit of their (short-lived) doubts. More of them might do so if a cheaper evening menu were available.

Main food style: Malaysian
Licensed: Yes
Tables: Smoking 6; Non–smoking 9
Approximate cost: £7 – £20
Cards: Access; AmEx; Diners; Visa
Open: M–F 12.00–14.00; M–T 18.00–23.00;
          F&Sat 18.00–23.30; Sun closed
Disabled access: No

MITCHELLS (West End)
31-35 Ashton Lane, G12   339 2220

In recognition of the growing importance of Byres Road as a centre of the culinary arts, Mitchells of North Street have opened this branch immediately facing the Ubiquitous Chip – such impudence! The site has had a chequered history. It was once the old Grosvenor restaurant which finally escaped from its time warp only to disappear (perhaps into another one?).

The new occupants are in a different league. The room itself has been completely redesigned (by a chap called Dey) in bright Caribbean style complete with Gaugin prints and decorative windows. Although tiny, the atmosphere is delightful – due partly to the friendly attitude of the staff. The menu is not too dissimilar to that of the Chip with lots of Scottish fish and game. Starters include Loch Fyne kipper terrine, gravad lax with mustard seed dressing and smoked trout. The main courses feature lobsters, venison, steak and quiche. The fillets of grey mullet in a saffron sauce were outstanding, as was the breast of duck with ginger sauce. Vegetables were not quite sufficient in quantity – more were brought (without hesitation or charge) on request. Desserts were irresistible but again not generous. Coffee was strong but without mints or refills. The overall impression was positive – this one could be heading for stardom.

Main food style: Scottish/French
Licensed: No (application pending)
Tables: Smoking 14; Non–smoking 0 (but segregated)
Approximate cost: £8 – £20
Cards: Most major cards
Open: M–S 12.00–14.30; 7 days 18.00–23.00
Disabled access: No

MURPH's BARRELHOUSE
10-14 Kelvinhaugh Street, G3   221 5569

The name Murphy is popping up all over the West
End. Experimentation seems to be the name of the
game. These establishments are essentially variations
on the pub 'n grub theme whether Indian, Italian or
Irish food is served. The risk is that they fall between
two stools. As you walk in, you are confronted with
what looks like a typical Glasgow stand-up bar,
complete with dedicated imbibers enjoying their
refreshment. After a double-take, you spot the tables
lining the side and rear walls. There's a good deal to
look at around you, from amusing slogans to
Hollywood photos.

The menu is unusual and features carefully selected
local produce. Sardines were expertly grilled and
served whole in a rich Livornese sauce with a plain
salad garnish. Soups and pastas won compliments, as
did the service. Different.

Main food style: International/Scottish
Licensed: Yes
Tables: Smoking 17; Non–smoking 0
Approximate cost: £7 – £15
Cards: All cards
Open: M–Sat 12.00–24.00;
         Sun 17.00–23.00 (No food)
Disabled access: Yes

OSCAR's BISTRO
562 Dumbarton Road, G11   337 1000

This is one of those 1950s style diners that gives the
casual passer-by the impression of a coke-and-coffee
burger joint.

The food is surprisingly wholesome and thoughtfully
presented. The snacky menu has the obligatory
croissants, baked potatoes and toasties (well-filled
and sprinkled with herbs), but the blackboard
specials aspire to higher things: asparagus with
lemon mayonnaise, mushrooms with cream and
paprika, rainbow trout Cleopatra, chicken supreme.
The steaks are big and juicy with garnishing to
match. Children are offered half-price main courses
and a short menu of their own. Enjoyable desserts
include banana fritters and ice cream.

Not a first choice for that special night out, perhaps,
but worth a visit all the same.

Main food style: British/International
Licensed: Yes
Tables: Smoking 9, Non–smoking 0
Approximate cost: £3.45 – £10
Cards: Access; AmEx; Visa
Open: M–W 09.00–18.00;
**   T–Sat 09.00–22.00 (last orders); Sun closed**
Disabled access: Yes

PJ's
Ruthven Lane, G12   339 0932

Over the years, this informal pastaria has
consolidated its reputation for low-cost, reliable
snacks. Refugees from the university canteens pour in
for the business lunch which offers a limited range
but superlative value. Overseas visitors enjoy the
frequent inclusion of Scottish produce (especially
fish) on the menu, although pastas are probably the
most accomplished dishes (and offered at a discount
at certain times). Soups are generally excellent.

The architecture of the dining room is such that you
may be seated in one of the semi-private nooks and
crannies. There's a non-smoking area. Service is
efficient and detached. Some of the diners are there
out of a nostalgic yearning for the late, great
Poachers which once occupied this site.

Main food type: Italian
Licensed: Yes
Tables: Smoking 16; Non–smoking 4
Approximate cost: £5 –£10
Cards: Access; Mastercard; Switch; Visa
Open: M–Sat 12.00–14.30, 17.00–23.00;
        Sun 12.00–23.00
Disabled access: Yes

La PARMIGIANA
447 Great Western Road, G12   334 0686

Clearly a ristorante nowadays, La Parmigiana has established a niche towards the upper end of the Italian market. The room is coolly elegant, with white table cloths and wooden chairs to match the panelled walls.

The lunch menu (£6.80) offers unexceptional but satisfying starters (soup of the day, minestrone, mozarella with tomatoes and basil, among others), while for the main course you may be offered rabbit, veal, fish or salad (all these items changing regularly). These are flawlessly cooked and decently presented. Desserts are ice cream or fruit salad. The evening menu is much more elaborate and priced accordingly: minestrone is £2.60, other starters go up to £5.60. Main courses are between £8 and £12, with many intriguing sounding fish dishes. Service was efficient if verging on the remote.

The higher prices may have sent some former customers off to nearby Trattoria Trevi, but this is the place to come for a more formal occasion.

Main food style: Italian
Licensed: Yes
Tables: Smoking 11; Non–smoking 0
Approximate cost: £7 – £25
Cards: All major cards
Open: M–Sat 12.00–14.30, 18.00–23.00; Sun closed
Disabled access: Yes, but toilets downstairs

The PARTHENON
725 Great Western Road, G12   334 6265

A dream site this for a restaurant – next to the BBC,
Glasgow University, Byres Road. The Parthenon has
exploited the opportunity well by providing a mix of
inexpensive budget menus (such as lunch for around
a fiver) and a range of ethnic Greek dishes for those
looking for an evening's entertainment. The room is
small and square with tables ruthlessly crammed
together.

The cooking is traditional with a light touch. Bean
soup or taramasalata are ideal starters. Thereafter, it's
up to you but think twice before passing over the
kebabs which are among the best in the city. Fish is
not always so deftly handled, but chat to the staff
who will give you fair advice. At one time, the
waiters behaved like escapees from a troupe of
whirling dervishes, but the Cafe Serghei on the South
Side appears to have signed the more frenetic ones
on. A great place for an office night out, but a
hopeless one for a romantic assignation.

Main food style: Greek
Licensed: Yes
Tables: Smoking 19; Non–smoking 0
Approximate cost: £6 – £17
Cards: All except AmEx
Open: M–Sat 12.00–14.30, 18.00–23.00;
**   Sun 18.00–22.30**
Disabled access: None

La PATISSERIE FRANCOISE
138a Byres Road, G12   334 1882

Certainly not a restaurant or even a conventional
cafe, this is more or less a shop with tables. Owned
by the same management as Passticceria Francois in
the Italian Centre, the baking here has always been
outstanding (choux-choux cake is heavenly) and long
may it continue.

Coffee and teas are excellent, as they have to be to
match the subtleties of the exquisite pastries, tarts
and gateaux. There are a few light snacks available
so you can eat lunch of a sort. These could do with
more thoughtful presentation – a cheese sandwich
with salad garnishing needs more room than a tiny
tea plate provides. (Maybe they are founding a
Crockery Conservation Society?) Staff are chatty.
Larger and more comfortable premises (and plates)
would work wonders.

Main food style: French/British
Licensed: No
Tables: Smoking 5; Non–smoking 0
Approximate cost: £5 – £8
Cards: None
Open: M–Sat 09.30–18.30; Sun closed
Disabled access: Yes

PIERRE VICTOIRE
16 Byres Road, G11   339 2544

On the site of the former Barcelona restaurant, this is
yet another branch of Pierre's rapidly expanding
empire. Opinions are deeply divided about these
places run on a franchise system with each branch
given a good deal of leeway when it comes to menu-
planning and even cooking. Meanwhile, the punters
are turning up in ever increasing numbers.

Certainly this Pierre Victoire is at the better end of the
spectrum. Its seating capacity is small giving the
kitchen more time for each order. The three course
lunch is wonderful value for a fiver. Creamy onion
and mushroom soup was exquisite (served with
sliced baguette), terrine de maison was smooth and
distinctive without being too tangy; chicken with
mustard sauce was marginally overcooked (the right
side to err on), carrots, potatoes and red cabbage
were lightly cooked and seasoned. Of the desserts,
glazed apple pie and cream had a light crisp pastry
and a decent quantity of fruit. The evening menu
looks strong on fish (steamed monkfish with spinach
pasta is £8.60) but problematic for vegetarians. Given
the shortage of plain French cooking in Glasgow, a
welcome new arrival.

Main food style: French
Licensed: Yes
Tables: Smoking 12; Non–smoking 0
Approximate cost: £5 – £14
Cards: All major cards except AmEx
Open: M–Sat 12.00–15.00, 18.00–23.00;
        Sun 12.30–15.00, 17.30–22.00
Disabled access: Yes

Il PESCATORE

148 Woodlands Road, G3   333 9239

Woodlands Road is the corridor linking the city
centre with the West End and is the obvious location
for the creation of a wining and dining precinct. That
may never happen, but Il Pescatore is likely to
continue to provide excellent fish and seafood meals
for as long as there are discerning Glaswegians to eat
them.

The consistency of this small Italian restaurant is
extraordinary. The fish is fresh and they know how
to bring out its flavours and textures to the full.
Garnishings are always generous. Soups and desserts
frame the main courses perfectly.

The wine list is more than adequate. And you get all
this with a smile and an affordable bill. Probably the
most underrated restaurant in Glasgow.

Main food style: Italian Seafood
Licensed: Yes
Tables: Smoking 12; Non–smoking 0
Approximate cost: £10 – £20
Cards: All major cards
Open: M–F 12.00–14.00; M–Sat 18.00–23.00;
    Sun closed
Disabled access: Yes, but toilets downstairs

La RIVIERA
147 Dumbarton Road, G11   334 8494

Partick Cross may have the world's highest
concentration of public houses per square metre. If
you can negotiate your way through the alcoholic
haze you'll discover one or two good eating places.
La Riviera has such a narrow frontage that you could
miss it by blinking. Once inside, you find yourself
facing a surprisingly long, narrow room. The effect is
cheering: there are hanging flowers, a dazzling mural
and partially cubicalised tables.

A two-course lunch or pre-theatre menu at £5.95 is
available all week; young children have a menu at
£3.25. The choice is formidable – around 17 starters
and 20 main courses. For an alternative to
minestrone, try pappa al pomodoro. Fish, meat and
vegetarian antipasta are all enjoyable. Noteworthy
main dishes include mixed goujon of fish, mixed
vegetables on rice, or any of the daily chef
specialities. Desserts are variable: try crespelle
deliziose (hot crepe filled with toffee ice cream) or
zuppa Italia (sponge soaked in marsala and maple
syrup). The celebration menu for two (£32.50) is a
sumptuous affair representing terrific value. There are
few weak points in cooking, service or general
ambience. A sound choice for an evening out.

Main food style: Italian
Licensed: Yes
Tables: Smoking 21; Non–smoking 0
Approximate cost: £7 – £20
Cards: Access; AmEx; Diners; Visa
Open: Sun–T 12.00–14.15, 17.30–22.15;
        F&Sat 12.00–14.15, 17.30–22.30
Disabled access: Yes

SHISH MAHAL
1348 Maryhill Road, G20   946 4243

The original Shish of Gibson Street was adored by the generation of Glasgwegians who pioneered the eating of curries. Since then, it has undergone two reincarnations – one in Park Road (the old Taj Mahal building), the other, more recently, next to Maryhill Police Station.

The new joint is a more ornate and glitzy affair than its predecessors (with an attended car park round the back). Climbing into your upholstered cubicle, you half expect the thing to take off, fairground-style, and whirl you round the room. The menu is lengthy and its content as easy on the palate as is the decor on the eye. A single pakora portion was sufficient for two and was served with two contrasting sauces. Chicken Tikka Burryani was tender, smooth and mildly spiced, while the Vegetable Patia brought no complaints. The fried rice had a curiously gelatinous texture – maybe that was intentional. Tea with Pakistani herbs is a refreshingly novel closer. Staff are anxious to please and build up a regular following.

An asset to this corner of the city.

Main food style: Indian
Licensed: Yes
Tables: Smoking 25; Non–smoking 0
Approximate cost: £8 – £14
Cards: Access; AmEx; Diners; Visa
Open: Sun–T 17.00–23.00; F&Sat 17.00–23.30
Disabled access: No

The TEA GARDEN
9 Gardner Street, G11   339 9174

This colourful and amusing little cafe is wedged
between a doctor's surgery and a Chinese takeaway
just off Dumbarton Road. The doll's house decor and
patterned table cloths combine attractively and lure
passers-by in off the street in droves.

The menu is predictable (except for the sandwich
section, which demands an extra 10p a portion for
brown bread – is this a joke?) There are a couple of
blackboard specials. Minestrone soup was piping hot
and tasted marvellous, although the ingredients may
or may not have been entirely fresh. Sandwiches and
baked potatoes are generously garnished with salad.
The desserts are all tempting: Dutch apple pie was a
joy, with light and crispy pastry and suitably moist
apples and raisins as a filling. Coffee seems to be of
variable quality and comes in cups (60p) or mugs
(75p). Tea can be brewed in various flavours. Staff
were pleasant, but the humming waitress was more
attentive to the background music than to her
customers. A notch down maybe from the nearby
Mariner, but fun all the same.

Main food style: British
Licensed: No
Tables: Smoking 10; Non–smoking 2
Approximate cost: £3 – £6
Cards: None
Open: M–Sat 09.00–17.00; Sun 11.30–16.30
Disabled access: Yes

TRATTORIA TREVI
526 Great Western Road, G12   334 3262

Unlike the soave La Parmigiana across the road, Trevi is informal in true trattoria fashion. The room is decorated with Italian footballing bric-a-brac and the floor slopes (downwards from West to East).

For under £6, you can eat a hearty three course lunch. Each course includes a Trevi Suprezza about which the waiter will enlighten you. The pastas have that soft, yielding texture normally only encountered in the Bologna region. Fish is expertly cooked and comes garnished with lashings of salad and fresh vegetables. Coffee was good but not refilled. The set evening menu (£16.50 for three courses) explores fish, poultry and veal territory in more detail. The choice is not large but you can wander into the a la carte alternatives if you prefer. The house white wine is dry and fruity and moderately priced.

The staff work under severe pressure at busy times but service does not suffer too drastically. Trevi has crept up on the Italian scene almost unnoticed. More widespread recognition is inevitable.

Main food style: Italian
Licensed: Yes
Tables: Smoking 10; Non-smoking 0
Approximate cost: £6 – £20
Cards: Access; Eurocard; Mastercard; Visa
Open: M–F 12.00–14.30, 17.30–23.00; S 17.00–23.00;
**   Sun 17.30–23.00**
Disabled access: Yes, but toilet downstairs

TWO FAT LADIES

88 Dumbarton Road, G11   339 1944

Whether through inverted snobbery or a misguided determination to deter the more genteel type of diner, the transport cafe image of this extraordinary restaurant has been strenuously preserved. Yet the cooking is as brilliantly accomplished as ever.

Two wall menus, one at a mere £8.88 (get it?) for two courses, were packed with exotic temptations: fish soup (apparently shellfish free), globe artichokes, salmon and hake patties, red snapper, mullet – each one of these will astonish and delight. There is a rare combination of thoughtfulness, precision and sheer inspiration about the selection, preparation and presentation of every aspect of the meal. Accompaniments of vegetables, sweet potatoes and plain salad are unfussy and avoid swamping the focal point of the dish. Desserts are not all quite in the same league, but the staff will give you an honest opinion.

The wine list contains some classy New Zealand labels which are a natural choice for this location. Highly recommended.

Main food style: International/Seafood/Vegetarian
Licensed: Yes
Tables: Smoking 9; Non–smoking 0
Approximate cost: £10 – £25
Cards: All except AmEx
Open: T–Sat 18.30–22.30; Sun–M closed
Disabled access: Yes

UBIQUITOUS CHIP
12 Ashton Lane, G12   334 5007

Insiders say that the kitchen of the Chip is in a class of its own. Undoubtedly, its imaginative use of local produce, the brilliance of the menu planning and the sheer technical skill of the cooking are a match for anyone anywhere in the UK. Strangely, the end result – the food on the plate – does not always impress the diner quite as much as you feel it should.

The unique covered courtyard setting becomes more extravagantly overgrown with vegetation with each passing year. The listed dishes roll off the tongue like poetry: shellfish bisque with cream and fresh ginger, flan of peat smoked haddies on a curried lentil base with peach sauce, fillets of Ayr landed cod on a bed of clapshot with roasted peppers and chilli oil, marinaded haunch of Inverness-shire venison with baked porridge cakes and a compote of fresh fruit. (These come from a set menu for £24.50 – three courses and coffee).

You are virtually guaranteed top quality but occasionally quantity can disappoint. At last, a set lunch (£11.50 for two courses and coffee) has been introduced but only at weekends. The wine list is legendary. Upstairs at the Chip is a less expensive but more mundane option for both lunch and dinner.

Main food style: Scottish
Licensed: Yes
Tables: Smoking 40; Non-smoking 0
Approximate cost: £15 – £29
Cards: All major cards
Open: M–Sat 12.00–14.30, 17.30–23.00;
        Sun 12.30–14.30, 18.30–23.00
Disabled access: Yes

UNDERGROUND GALLERY
2 Cresswell Lane, G12   339 0968

Despite the name, this is not primarily an art gallery
although there are frequently changing exhibits on
the walls. The unprepossessing entrance to this much
admired basement cafe is notable for a bizarre
collection of posters advertising everything from yoga
classes to adventure holidays.

The self-service counter has to be negotiated with
painful slowness at peak times, but the patience of
the customers testifies to the excellent quality of the
food including home-made quiches, salads, pastas
and (renowned) baking. Vegetable soup is a
justifiable favourite, especially in winter. The hot
morning scones are highly prized and combine
perfectly with the excellent coffee. Not desperately
cheap (main courses are around £3 – £4) but neither
are the ingredients.

The cheerless staff looked as if they needed a good
holiday. Here's a puzzle: non-smokers are banished
to a smallish separate room away from the service
area. Surely it is the smokers who should be
quarantined?

Main food style: British/International
Licensed: No
Tables: Smoking 17; Non-smoking 12
Approximate cost: £4 – £7
Cards: None
Open: M–Sat 09.00–18.00; Sun 10.30–18.00
Disabled access: No

WEST END PIANO BAR
Grosvenor Hotel, G12   339 8811

This former Stakis Steakhouse has transformed itself
into an altogether posher establishment. The room
itself is fascinating with its island bar flanked by a
sweeping curve of stained glass. Service is polished
without being obsequious. Taped musack is
mercifully subdued – you only get the live pianist in
the evening.

The lunchtime buffet is astonishing value at £4.95 for
two courses (starter and main). Egg Florentine was a
delight, artistically presented with multicoloured
sauces; the broth was full-bodied, lightly seasoned
and piping hot. The array of choices at the carvery is
formidable – poultry, game, pork, fish, cold meats
and salads. The venison fricassee was a mite on the
tough side, the roast turkey succulent and tender.
Baked trout was superb. Vegetables were fresh,
plentiful and expertly cooked. Coffee was refilled,
unprompted (which is fair enough at £1.25). A
triumphant opening spell, but can the standard be
maintained?

Main food style: American/International
Licensed: Yes
Tables: Smoking 23; Non–smoking 12
Approximate cost: £5 – £24
Cards: All cards
Open: M–Sun 12.00–23.00
Disabled access: Yes

WICKETS HOTEL
52 Fortrose Street, G11   334 9334

Perched on a hillside the name of this hotel is
presumably derived from a nearby cricket ground.
There are mixed reports of the lunch (around £10)
and dinner (around £14) served in the Conservatory
Restaurant – which really is housed in a conservatory,
and a rather splendid one at that.

The real forte of Wickets is to be found at the rear of
the upstairs bar called Randalls. For there you will
discover something rare and precious in this part of
the world – a lovely secluded beer garden.
Admittedly, the summer temperatures seldom rise
sufficiently to make eating al fresco a thrilling
prospect. But when they do, it's a sheer delight to sit
outdoors sipping your drink and munching your
meal – even if it's only a toastie. In reality, Scottish
attitudes as well as the weather explain our collective
reluctance to eat in the open. We should demand
more such facilities and restaurants will provide
them. At Wickets, the whole business is rather half-
hearted: you can eat outside, but you have to order
your food in advance at the bar, and you can only
have snacks.

Perhaps this is a result of our licensing laws, in which
case they should be amended forthwith. Two cheers,
then, for the Wickets – at least you tried.

Main food style: British/International
Licensed: Yes
Tables: Smoking 35; Non–smoking 0; Outside 45
Approximate cost: £6 – £17
Cards: All major cards
Open: M–Sat 12.00–22.30; Sun 12.30–21.30
Disabled access: None

THE CITY CENTRE

Glasgow City Centre covers the main shopping,
commercial and entertainment districts. Sauchiehall
Street runs from the top end of Buchanan Street (at
the Royal Concert Hall) westwards all the way to the
University. Buchanan Street contains the renowned
Princes Square shopping mall. The lower end of
Buchanan Street meets the enormously popular
Argyle Street. All of these are part-pedestrianised.
Most of the theatres, cinemas and art galleries are to
be found around the central and eastern part of
Sauchiehall Street. Lovers of fine Victorian
architecture should explore this area street by street.

L'ARIOSTO
92 Mitchell Street, G1   221 0971/8543

There is an old-fashioned plushness about this upmarket Italian restaurant. Booths provide a welcome respite from fellow human beings. (If you want more intimate contact, book a table for the weekend dinner dance – but it's advisable to bring a partner).

The set three course lunch (£7.50) is superb value, and the waiters will do a fantastic job racing you through it if you are unfortunate enough to be in a hurry. The Egg Florentine starter is massive – and tastes good to boot. Sole goujon, veal chops, vegetarian dishes – all can be recommended. The main menu is formidable: five kinds of soup (including cream lobster bisque at £4.10), eight (or more) varieties of fish from fried or grilled sole (£7.35) to scampi alla Scozese (£12.50). Tournedos Rossini (£14) has a high reputation here. Vegetables are delicious and cleverly selected – but you are charged extra for them (always a mean trick). Desserts are pretty good too – especially the moist and rich torta della casa. The wine list is suitably extensive, but keep a watchful eye on the prices of the classics. There really isn't a weak department – with the painful exception of your personal financial state by the time you've finished your last cup of espresso.

Main food style: Italian
Licensed: Yes
Tables: Smoking 30; Non–smoking 6
Approximate cost: £8 – £30
Cards: All major cards
Open: M–Sat 12.00–14.30, 17.30–23.00; Sun closed
Disabled access: Yes

BABY GRAND
3-7 Elmbank Gardens G2   248 4942

Too many bar-cafes in Glasgow stop serving food in the early evening. Not so Baby Grand which allows you to eat after midnight – a boon to theatre or cinema goers who become peckish after the performance.

The long and narrow shape of the place must be an architect's nightmare, but the space is cleverly used and the recent refurbishment has worked well.

The breadth of choice – from coffee and cake to a four courser – is a further attraction. Sandwiches are well-garnished and the more substantial dishes (such as swordfish steak, fondues, pastas) are worthy of respect. The pianist contributed intermittently and unenthusiastically – hardly surprising given the apparent indifference of the vast majority of the customers. The staff perform miraculous contortions in the tight confines behind the bar – an entertainment in itself.

Main food style: British/International
Licensed: Yes
Tables: Smoking 15; Non–smoking 0
Approximate cost: £5 – £12
Cards: Access; Visa
Open: M–T 08.00–24.00; F&Sat 08.00–01.00;
         Sun 08.00–24.00
Disabled access: No

BRASSERIE
176 West Regent Street G2   248 3801

Having started life as an offshoot of the once-revered
Rogano, the Brasserie has matured to the point
where many consider that it now stands head-and-
shoulders above its parent institution in terms of food
quality and value for money. The menu is flexible
enough to cope with the demands of pre-theatre,
late-night and all-evening customers.

Because local produce features prominently, visitors
love the experience. Wild mushrooms in garlic butter
are a joy, the soups are superb. Fish and poultry are
cooked to perfection and lovingly presented. Portions
could have been more generous – that extra 10-15%
can make all the difference. The wine list is classy,
the cafetiere coffee unrivalled. The staff know their
job and have a relaxed, informal attitude which
permeates their surroundings. The near blackout
lighting is controversial – some rethinking of this
might pay dividends. Heating has been known to fail
to cope adequately with winter weather.
Nevertheless, the verdict is clear: one to return to
again and again. Highly recommended.

Main food style: French/British/Scottish
Licensed: Yes
Tables: Smoking 22; Non–smoking 0
Approximate cost: £12 – £20
Cards: All cards
Open: M–F 12.00–23.00 (last orders);
       Sat 12.00–15.00, 17.00–23.00; Sun closed
Disabled access: No

The BELFRY
652 Argyle Street G3   221 0630

Adjoining The Buttery (and sharing the kitchen) is an altogether more modest establishment which has achieved a distinctive style of its own. The interior looks as though it must have been constructed from bits of demolished churches – there are pews, stained glass and bookshelves containing dusty volumes. The bare floor boards are excessively stark – maybe this is temporary.

The menu is small but interesting. Soup is invariably outstanding and for starters there are several enticing options: pasta with honeyed ham, broccoli and nuts (£2.65), julienne of vegetables with herbs and smoked fish cream (£3.60). Main courses span fish (mackerel and spinach, skate wing with a prawn and caper butter), game (venison stew finished with blackcurrants and sour cream), beef and lamb – all around £7 to £9, fully garnished. There are blackboard specials also. Finish up with wonderful home-made peach and mint ice cream (£2.55) and "unlimited" coffee. Service is courteous. The low beams and compact floor space may feel a bit oppressive on a busy evening. Perhaps not in the same league as its prestigious neighbour, this is a good choice for high quality food in unusual surroundings at tolerable prices.

Main food style: British
Licensed: Yes
Tables: Smoking 14; Non–smoking 0
Approximate cost: £12 – £17
Cards: All major cards
Open: M–F 12.00–14.30, 18.00–23.00; Sat 18.00–23.00;
      Sun closed
Disabled access: No

The BUTTERY

652 Argyle Street, G3   221 8188

Glasgow without The Buttery would be like Paris
without Maxime's – inconceivable. The building is a
magnificent Victorian tenement (have you noticed the
gargoyles?) which houses the most elegant restaurant
in the city. The Oyster Bar is a comfortable place to
relax with a drink while you study the menu – if you
can take your eyes off the riveting artefacts on the
ceilings, walls and bookshelves. The main dining
room, with its wood panels and discreet partitions, is
equally delightful.

The emphasis of the food remains firmly on fish,
seafood and game. The dishes are gorgeous. Starters
include a platter of homesmoked seafood with
saffron mayonnaise (£5.10), terrine of venison,
pigeon and pistachio nut with sun-dried tomato
marmalade (£4.95). Main courses, with prices quoted
excluding vegetables, include pan-fried fillets of sole
and trout in herb batter with ratatouille (£12.60),
shallow fried mignons of venison with raisin and
oatmeal farce on a caraway jus (£13.95). The wines
are superb. Desserts are legendary, if you can cope
with them. Coffee comes with home-made petits
fours. Service is charming. If you're bent on sheer
self-indulgence, this is the address.

Main food style: British/Scottish
Licensed: Yes
Tables: Smoking 17 (no pipes or cigars);
        Non–smoking 0
Approximate cost: £15 – £30
Cards: All major cards
Open: M–F 12.00–14.30, 19.00–22.30;
        Sat 19.00–22.30; Sun closed
Disabled access: Yes

CAFE ROYAL (Theatre Royal)
Hope Street, G2   332 1370

The Theatre Royal desperately needed a proper cafe-bar to service hungry theatre-goers but you don't have to be bopping to Boheme to eat there. The name is unfortunate with its connotations of the Victorian splendour associated with other establishments. The room has dark wood-panelling and theatrical paintings on the walls. Classical background music (what else?) is just audible above the buzz of conversation.

You must book if you want a pre-theatre meal, but there is an all-day menu which includes lentil soup (£1.85), apple and walnut salad (£2.65), vegetable stroganoff (£4.75), beef bourgignonne and rice (£4.95). Other lighter possibilities are filled croissants or baguettes, and a tapas selection. Desserts are sweet and sticky (profiteroles, chocolate thunder cake – both £2.50).

All very fresh, nicely presented and a happy addition to the theatre complex. Thought could be devoted to a more imaginative use of the limited floor space.

Main food style: International
Licensed: Yes
Tables: Smoking 10; Non–smoking 0
Approximate cost: £8 – £12
Cards: None (at the moment!)
Disabled access: Yes

CAPRESE
217 Buchanan Street, G2   332 3070

The top end of Buchanan Street is a problem. Its gradual deterioration might have been halted by the opening of the Royal Concert Hall but hasn't. The recession killed off plans for the development of a new department store which would have injected new life in the area. Sooner or later it will revive, being so close to the centre of things, and the restaurant trade will no doubt play its part.

Currently, there are depressingly few reliable eating places for concert goers to choose from. The Caprese is one of them. The red check table cloths, the curios on the walls, the ebullience of the staff and the plain but tasty Italian cooking are among the reasons for its popularity.

The traditional menu items are all there and are acceptably cooked, but the chef comes to life if you order something more challenging – veal cordon bleu for example. The house wine has improved in recent times.

Main food style: Italian
Licensed: Yes
Tables: Smoking 16 (no pipes); Non–smoking 0
Approximate cost: £6 – £16
Cards: Access; AmEx; Diners
Open: M–F 12.00–14.30, 17.30–23.00;
         Sat 17.30–23.00; Sun closed
Disabled access: No

The CHAPTER HOUSE
26 Bothwell Street, G2   221 8913

The front section of this popular little cafe is a
bookshop (Pickering and Inglis). The cafe is to be
found at the rear, on a slightly raised area. The
seating is comfortable and the food enjoyable without
being in any way exciting. The Chapter House salad
is a good buy (£3.50) with its nourishing mixture of
tuna, celery and fruit. Wholemeal sandwiches are
fresh and moist. Other sound choices are lasagna and
baked potato.

The baking is especially recommended: scones,
shortbread and a lovely lemon meringue pie. Coffee
is fine, and the soft drinks include rarities such as
Purdeys Elixir.

Prices are competitive – soup and a sandwich would
deprive you of a mere £2.60. On the (two) hot days
in the summer, you can sit outside on the pavement
and admire the traffic roaring towards the city centre.

Main food style: British
Licensed: No
Tables: Smoking 5; Non–smoking 10
Approximate cost: £4 – £6
Cards: Access; Visa; Switch
Open: M–F 08.30–16.30; Sat 09.00–16.30;
        Sun closed
Disabled access: Yes

CHINATOWN
42 New City Road, G4   353 0037

This newish restaurant is part of a Chinese shopping
complex tucked underneath the M8 adjacent to
Garnethill where a large Chinese community resides.
In the evenings, parking is easier than during the
day. On entering the dining room, the visual impact
is powerful – huge picture windows, sumptuous
fittings, pink damask tablecloths and napkins, and
pretty porcelain china. Watch the trick the waiter
performs as he opens your packet of chopsticks.

The menu is huge, but not everything on it will
necessarily be available. The food is tasty and
plentiful. There are some unusual dishes – soup with
noodles, mixed hors d'oevres (seaweed, spring rolls,
chicken and beef satay, spare ribs, sesame toast).
Duck was crisp on the outside, tender on the inside
but the flavour was almost overwhelmed by a
pungent sauce. Fried shredded fillet steak with salted
vegetables was excellent. As well as a comprehensive
wine list, Chinese Tsing Tao beer is stocked. Desserts
are mountainous.

A distinctly promising newcomer. Its location should
ensure that the kitchen will strive to satisfy even the
tastes of discerning Chinese customers.

Main food style: Cantonese
Licensed: Yes
Tables: Smoking 35; Non–smoking 0
Approximate cost: £7 – £20
Cards: All major cards
Open: 7 days 12.00–24.00
Disabled access: Yes

CIAO by EQUI
441-445 Sauchiehall Street, G2   332 4565

The front section looks like a run-of-the-mill ice cream parlour. The main dining room is a large, beautifully proportioned rectangle complete with chandelier and gallery. By day, the resonant acoustics hum to heated conversation and combine with the aroma of expresso to remind one of an exclusive Roman coffee house. By night, the ambience is infinitely more subdued.

The budget meals (lunch at £4.95 and pre-theatre at £7.95) are tempting, but the portions look smaller than those ordered a la carte. While the range is vast, pastas are a delight and the pizzas are outstanding: thin based with exquisite toppings such as Tropicana (pineapple, sweetcorn, banana), Veneziana (prawns and mussels) and Vegeteriana (self-explanatory). Desserts were variable. Straight coffee was much preferable to the thin cappuccino. Staff are hospitable in the Italian tradition. You can buy a Pinocchio model on the way out.

Main food style: Italian/British
Licensed: Yes
Tables: 35; Non–smoking (catered for)
Approximate cost: £5 – £20
Cards: All major cards
Open: M–T 10.30–15.00, 17.00–23.00;
       F 10.30–15.00; Sat 11.00–15.00;
       F&Sat 17.00–24.00; Sun closed
Disabled access: Yes, but toilets downstairs

CRANNOG
28 Cheapside Street, G3   221 1727

A crannog was a fortified island on which a self-contained community existed and made its living from fishing. Crannog Scottish Seafoods are a fishing and seafood marketing company who run two restaurants of which this is one (the other is in Fort William). Although visible from the Kingston Bridge, finding the place is tricky.

No matter – if you appreciate freshly caught fish or seafood, expertly cooked and nicely presented, seek out the Crannog. You will not be disappointed. The lunch menu (£7.50) is displayed on large blackboards brought to your table. There are several choices of starters (or soup) and main courses. Bouillabaisse (£2.95 a la carte) is magnificent: rich and hearty as they come, and substantial enough for you to consider going straight on to dessert. Cod steak was tender and delicately seasoned, herring in oatmeal was beautifully cooked but the oatmeal batter could have been lighter. Accompaniments were lightly cooked potatoes and carrots and a colourful salad. Three cheers for the basket of bread and the jug of Loch Katrine Nectar brought unsolicited. You can order a decent half-bottle of white wine. Coffee was excellent but no refills were offered. A rare treat from an imaginative enterprise. Highly recommended.

Main food style: Scottish/Seafood
Licensed: Yes
Tables: Smoking 14; Non–smoking 0
Approximate cost: £8.50 – £20
Cards: Access; Mastercard; Switch; Visa
Open: T–Sat 12.00–14.30; T–T 17.30–21.30 (last
      orders); F&S 17.30–22.30; Sun closed
Disabled access: No

D'ARCYS
Princes Square, G1   226 4309

Since the opening of this most exclusive of shopping malls, D'Arcys has become a meeting place for flamboyant youngsters who would have been called yuppies in the 1980s and who look more than a little bemused by the 1990s. As well as being addicted to loud taped pop music, they express their aspirations to sophistication through ostentatious public eating.

The imaginative menu spans the globe: French, Italian, Chinese and Mexican dishes are represented. Starter prices are high: deep fried camembert (£3.95), prawn cocktail (£4.95) but you get a decent plateful. The main courses include colourful stirfries and salads (£5 -£7) and represent better value than the open sandwiches. The eye-popping desserts (around £3 – £4) will defeat most appetites. There are irritating rules, like a minimum charge of £4 per head at lunchtime, or the insistence on self-service alcohol at the outside tables (arising from the Scottish licensing laws apparently).

Main food style: International
Licensed: Yes
Tables: Smoking 38; Non–smoking 12
Approximate cost: £10 – £20
Cards: Access; AmEx; Delta; Diners; Mastercard;
           Switch; Visa
Open: M–Sat 09.00–24.00; Sun 11.30–17.30
Disabled access: Yes

DINO's
39-41 Sauciehall Street, G2   332 0626

The eastern segment of the Sauciehall Street precinct adjoins the Royal Concert Hall and could easily support half a dozen quality eating places. For some reason, Dino's has virtually the whole patch to itself – a monopoly which may have bred a certain amount of complacency.

The menu is disappointingly limited in range, the pizzas and pastas being the main attractions. The food itself was not tremendously memorable, either qualitatively or quantitatively although it was unfussily cooked and presented. Nevertheless, it does fulfil an important function either as a pretheatre or as a late night snack.

There is something endearing about the place. If you are in a hurry, the service can be spectacularly swift. At peak times, the restaurant can be packed out, but the staff will do their best to fit you in. During the concert season, you should be able to spot members of the Scottish National Orchestra replenishing expended calories after the performance.

Main food style: Italian
Licensed: Yes
Tables: Smoking 30; Non-smoking 0
Approximate cost: £5 – £20
Cards: All major cards except Switch
Open: M–T 12.00–23.00; F&S 12.00–24.00;
       Sun 12.00–23.00
Disabled access: Yes

FRATELLI SARTI
133 Wellington Street, G2   248 2228

Remember Fazzis of Cambridge Street? That still exists but the mantle of greatness has been passed to the Fratelli Sarti which is reminiscent of Fazzis in its early days. There's either a bar counter or small tables to sit at, and you don't usually have the luxury of being able to choose. This is Italy in Glasgow – the customers unconsciously adopt Italian accents, so authentic is the atmosphere.

The deli has the usual selection of cheeses and salamis which are the perfect backdrop for cafe eating. Pictures of Lucca adorn the walls. The menu is limited, but this scarcely matters.

The pizzas are delicious, with paper thin bases and generous toppings. Cakes and coffee are wonderful. The staff are extrovert – watch how they get the wine down from the upper reaches of the shelves. Glorious stuff – the place should have a conservation order slapped on it.

Main food style: Italian
Licensed: Yes
Tables: Smoking 6; Non–smoking 6
Approximate cost: £7 – £10
Cards: Access; Switch; Visa; Vouchers
Open: M–Sat 08.00–22.00; Sun closed
Disabled access: Yes, but no disabled toilets

HILTON Hotel
1 William Street, G3   204 5555

The spanking new Hilton Hotel has a number of
unusual features, including a grand piano in the
lobby which appears to play itself. There are two
restaurants: the deli-style Minsky's and the posher
Cameron's.

Minsky's had its share of gremlins shortly after
opening but these seem to have been more or less
banished. The design is marvellous – a series of
interconnecting rooms all beautifully decked out with
olde worlde features. At some of the tables you get
the impression of total privacy. Staff are rapidly
gaining in confidence and much-needed polish –
their amiability was never in question. The buffet
menu is terrific and represents better value than the a
la carte. You help yourself to cold meats, salads, fish
and vegetables. All look tempting, although the range
of dishes could be expanded a little. Desserts are
triumphant and there is plentiful coffee or tea.

Cameron's is the new home of master chef Ferrier
Richardson (remember October?); his many admirers
hope that he has successfully imported his renowned
skill and flair to the city centre. Rather like the new
conductor of an orchestra, he may take time to
acclimatise, but early reports are strongly favourable.
Reactions to the prices are rather less glowing.

Main food style: American/British
Licensed: Yes
Tables: Minsky's Smoking 22; Non-smoking 22
Approximate cost: £17 – £35
Cards: All major cards
Open: 7 days 06.30–10.30, 12.00–23.00
Disabled access: Yes

The JENNY Traditional Tea Rooms
18-20 Royal Exchange Square, G1   204 4988

The neo-classical elegance of Royal Exchange Square demands something special and Jenny provides it. The visual impact is striking: olde worlde charm lightened with bright floral patterns adorning tables inside and (optimistically) out. Smokers are sent to their own patch.

The menu offers 2-in-1 pies, savoury buns and other frightfully English-sounding delicacies. Toppings and fillings are mind-boggling: smoked salmon and cream cheese (goes well on a baked potato), pastrami and piccalilli, cottage cheese and fresh strawberries. Sticky toffee pudding is a world beater. The Jenny Gateau Tea (£3.25) or simpler Jenny Tea (£2.95) are less expensive alternatives to the lunch. You have a choice of 9 types of tea (95p a pot) but Coke addicts will have to go elsewhere for their fix.

On Thursdays, Fridays and Saturdays an evening "Taste of Scotland" dinner (broth, haggis and the like) will doubtless pull in English visitors – Glaswegians are more likely to opt for the less familiar sassenach fodder.

Main food style: Scottish/British
Licensed: Yes
Tables: Smoking 12; Non–smoking 48
Approximate cost: £4 – £16
Cards: Access; AmEx; Diners; Visa
Open: M–W 08.00–19.00; T–Sat 08.00–21.00;
        Sun 11.00–18.00
Disabled access: Yes

LOON FUNG
417 Sauchiehall Street, G2   332 1240

The Loon Fung is widely considered to be the best
Chinese restaurant in Glasgow. Certainly it's the most
authentic – even the customers are Chinese. A
somewhat dreary dining room is lightened by a
brightly coloured wall carving of a dragon and
phoenix which is guaranteed to fascinate children.

The menu may look unfamiliar to those who are
used to Anglo-Chinese eating. Dim Sum (dumpling)
is the speciality, with over 30 kinds to choose from.
Prawns, squids and oysters take up a good deal of
menu space and are said to be excellent. Other
recommended dishes are Cantonese roast duck
(£7.50) and sliced abalones with oyster sauce (priced
according to availability). If you feel up to it, you can
order a whole aromatic duck as an appetiser (£22).
There's a set lunch and various set dinners for two,
four or six. The vegetarian set dinner appears to have
9 courses (£11.50). The staff will advise on a number
of dishes not advertised on the menu: the mind
boggles as to the nature of these "under the counter"
delicacies. The automatic service charge may account
for reports of disinterested service.

Main food style: Chinese/Cantonese
Licensed: Yes
Tables: 30; Non–smokers catered for
Approximate cost: £6 – £25
Cards: All major cards
Open: 7 days 12.00–23.30
Disabled access: Yes, but no disabled toilet

Di MAGGIO's
21 Royal Exchange Square, G2   248 2111

Each Di Maggio branch has its individual personality.
This one is a flashy, streamlined version which caters
for the sophisticates of nearby Princes Squareland.
They do the usual range of pizzas and pastas, but
families often feel more at home in the basement cafe
(when open – usually until the early evening) which
has its own menu and blackboard specials – but no
pizzas!

There are no difficulties for vegetarians except that
the macaroni and cheese is liable to come with ham
unless you specify otherwise. Omelettes are
competent enough if not brilliant. Desserts are
exceptionally tasty – strawberry cheesecake and
lemon meringue pie vie with each other for honours
– but are a bit quantitatively challenged.

The upstairs room has much more space but is not as
attractively fitted as the cellar which, like the desserts,
could also be described as a bit wee. The waitress
service is cheerful and efficient.

Main food style: Italian
Licensed: Yes
Tables: Smoking 38, Non–smoking 12
Approximate cost: £5 – £10
Cards: All major cards except Diners
Open: M–T 12.00–14.30, 17.00–24.00;
**   F 12.00–14.30, 17.00–01.00;**
**   Sat 12.00–01.00; Sun 17.00–24.00**
Disabled access: Yes

MITCHELLS

157 North Street, G3   204 4312

When it first opened, Mitchells was hailed as a rival
to the Ubiquitous Chip and The Buttery. Despite
establishing a solid reputation and winning the
occasional award, its potential has never been fully
realised.

The upstairs bar offers superior snacks (open
sandwiches are particularly good) while the main
restaurant specialises in fish and game. All the dishes,
whether ordered upstairs or downstairs, are skilfully
prepared although quantities can be erratic. Starters
vary in price from garlic bread (£1) to smoked
salmon (£4.25). Of the main dishes, the "Bistro
Regulars" are excellent value: home-baked steak,
onion and mushroom pie, with vegetables, is £4.50;
vegetarian stir-fry with bean sprouts is £3.75. Of the
sweets, the bread and butter pudding (£2.45) and
chocolate fudge cake (£2.45) are in constant demand.

Since the transfer of some of the staff to the new
branch in Ashton Lane, there have been some
worries about the kitchen talents being too thinly
spread. One possibility is that North Street will
become more of a bistro-bar (a process already
underway judging by the latest menu) while the
serious cooking will migrate to the West End. Ideally,
high standards will be maintained in both.

Main food style: Scottish/International
Licensed: Yes
Tables: Smoking 18; Non-smoking 0
Approximate cost: £7 – £20
Cards: Most major cards
Open: M–Sat 12.00–23.00/24.00; Sun closed
Disabled access: Yes

NICO's
379 Sauchiehall Street, G2   332 5736

Nico's was one of the pioneers of the Glasgow cafe-bar genre and is arguably one of the best. Unlike many of its competitors, there is a very continental yet wholly unpretentious feeling about the place.

There are few more civilised ways of starting your day than with a Nico's breakfast of orange juice, freshly baked croissant with butter and jam and a pot of strong cafetiere coffee (£2.95). Lunch continues until 4pm. Croissants, baguettes, baked potatoes and rye bread sandwiches can be filled with a range of appetisingly fresh ingredients. First-class soup along with a baguette filled with tuna or cheese is good value (£2.95). There are changing daily specials.

Desserts are worth leaving room for – passion fruit cheesecake was sensational. On weekend evenings, the bar area becomes crowded – drinking takes over from eating as the dominant activity.

Main food style: International
Licensed: Yes
Tables: Smoking 16; Non-smoking 0
Approximate cost: £4 – £10
Cards: None
Open: M–S 08.00–24.00; Sun 12.00–24.00
Disabled access: Yes

NORTH ROTUNDA
28 Tunnel Street, G3   204 1238

The area around the Scottish Exhibition and
Conference Centre is punctuated by two striking
landmarks – the Moat House Hotel and the North
Rotunda. The Rotunda is a brilliant transformation of
a semi-derelict 19th century edifice into a restaurant
and bar complex.

The base of the building is a spacious pizzeria, the
middle is a sophisticated French affair, while the
dome has been turned into a futuristic cocktail bar
with spectacular views of the river.

The pizzeria is a favourite of families with children
who are lured by the attractive circular setting, the
100 plus pasta sauce variations and the cut-price early
evening meals. This is a lively, colourful place in
which you may see several sparkler-adorned birthday
cakes process their way to wide-eyed youngsters.

The French floor is rather formal and has a pleasing
tranquillity about it – no noisy birthday parties here –
but you have to be prepared to spend: the three
course lunch is £11.95 and the full evening dinner
£18.95. For this you get highly competent classical
French cuisine featuring lots of Scottish produce
reinforced with subtle sauces and flavourings.

Main food style: French/Italian
Licensed: Yes
Tables: Smoking 85; Non–smoking 0
Approximate cost: £8 – £25
Cards: Access; AmEx; Diners; Visa
Open: M–Sat 12.00–14.30, 17.00–23.00;
**   Sun 17.00–23.00**
Disabled access: Yes

PAPERINO's
283 Sauchiehall Street, G2   332 3800

This lively cafe-restaurant radiates a sense of fun,
Wherever you look there are smiles – from the faces
on the Parma football team (in the photo near the
entrance) to everyone else in the room – staff and
customers alike.

The atmosphere of sunny enjoyment is infectious,
which is a major reason why this pizza and pasta
parlour is so popular. The cubicalised seating is not
ideal for the long-legged. Otherwise the room is
comfortable if a little too brightly lit (although this
does enable you to see what you are eating).

The menu is short and unremarkable, but several
vegetarian options are helpfully highlighted. Fish is
not well represented outside of squid, mussels and
prawns. Desserts are rather interesting but expensive.
Young children can (and frequently do) eat half
portions. Definitely not a first choice for a night out,
but an excellent spot to fuel post-entertainment
appetites.

Main food style: Italian
Licensed: Yes
Tables: 20, No-smoking if required
Approximate cost: £9 – £15
Cards: Access; Diners; Visa; Vouchers
Open: M–T 12.00–15.00, 17.00–23.00;
**   F 12.00–15.00, 17.00–24.00;**
**   Sat 12.00–24.00; Sun closed**
Disabled access: Yes

PAVAROTTI TRATTORIA

91 Cambridge Street, G3   332 9713

This popular city centre restaurant, with a multi-storey car park conveniently opposite, continues to maintain high standards in the quality of culinary preparation. The personal attention by the owner to the comfort of each diner is refreshing and charming. The pleasingly relaxed surroundings, reminiscent of a Mediterranean enclosed courtyard, soothe and make time slip pleasantly by.

The daily lunch menu is excellent value, and the popularity of the set pre-theatre menu makes booking especially advisable whenever the Theatre Royal is open. In addition to the extensive a la carte menu, the daily "blackboard" of that day's pick of the market ensures the best of something for everyone; fish dishes being a particular speciality of the chef. A good selection of wines from all parts of Italy can compliment every dish.

A reliable choice for an enjoyable evening or for a special function.

Main food style: Italian
Licensed: Yes
Tables: Smoking 15, Non-smoking 0 but non-smokers
        can be segregated
Approximate cost: £5 – £21
Cards: All major cards
Open: M–S 12.00–14.30, 17.30–23.00; Sun 17.30–23.00
Disabled access: Yes, but restricted toilet access

SANNINO PIZZERIA
61 Elmbank Street, G2   332 3565

Both this Sannino and the more spacious one in Bath Street have built up a large regular clientele over the years by following the simple business principle of giving people what they want at prices they can afford.

The proximity of this basement restaurant to the Kings Theatre has also ensured the popularity of the low-priced pre-theatre menu. The choice is fairly limited by Italian standards. Soup and desserts are reliable, as are the pastas, but the pizzas are churned out endlessly with amazingly predictable quality. The bases are thin and yielding, the toppings generous. A tried and tested formula, perhaps, but it works every time.

No complaints about service. Accommodation is on the cramped side but the booth-style seating gives a degree of privacy. The house white wine can be cloyingly sweet.

Main food style: Italian
Licensed: Yes
Tables: 15 ; Non–smokers catered for
Approximate cost: £5 – £15
Cards: All major cards
Open: M–W 12.00–14.30, 17.00–23.00;
          T–Sat 12.00–14.30, 17.00–24.00;
          Sun 17.00–23.00
Disabled access: No

TGI FRIDAY's

113 Buchanan Street, G1   221 6996

Thank Goodness It's Here seems to be the prevailing popular opinion of Thank Goodness It's Friday. This is as American as they come in the West of Scotland and you know where you are as soon as the toothpaste smile in a uniform greets you enthusiastically at the door. All the same, there is a palpable excitement about the place which enlivens this corner of Buchanan Street.

The menu is enormous and child friendly. As expected, portions are generous and the food presented with all due razzmatazz: an omelette, for example, is bedecked with toast or muffin along with a pot of jam. Prices are high even if you choose light snacks and some of the steaks will set you back around £12. Favourite desserts include chocolate maltcake and ice cream, cheesecake and caramel pie – they must have an exclusive contract with a large sugar plantation.

Droves of care-worn businessmen pour in at lunchtime, lap up the ersatz attention from highly presentable young waitresses and emerge an hour later with a spring in their step. For those of us not on expenses, the size of the bill could have the opposite effect.

Main food style: American
Licensed: Yes
Tables: Smoking 40; Non–smoking 30
Approximate cost: £10 – £22
Cards: AmEx; Visa
Open: M–Sun 12.00–23.30
Disabled access: Yes

THE MERCHANT CITY AND EAST END

The Merchant City – wedged between the City Centre and the High Street – has only relatively recently seen a revival in its fortunes. The historic civic and commercial heart of the city, it boasts many fine buildings which have attracted a large number of residential developments in the last decade. At the upper end of the High Street is the delightful Cathedral Precinct including the new St Mungo Museum of Religious Art (housing Dali's masterpiece depicting The Crucifixion). Also in this area are Strathclyde University and the renascent East End.

BABBITY BOWSTER
16 Blackfriars Street, G1   552 5055

Babbity's is a unique institution. More than a pub, more than a restaurant, it's a centre of authentic Glasgow culture. It has been said that Babbity's is full of character – and characters. Journalists, lawyers, students – they're all equally at home here. The room is a period piece, with high ceilings and a fine open hearth. There are photographs of well-known Glasgow figures on the walls.

As for the food, the upstairs restaurant has never really taken off but the bar meals more than compensate. There are daily blackboard specials as well as the regular dishes: Loch Fyne mussels (£4.25), home-made cream of cauliflower soup (£1.25), stovies, haggis and neeps, croque monsieur (between £3 and £4). The coffee is good and the beer (real ale) better. On Sunday, you can pore over newspapers while consuming brunch. At weekends, the scene resembles a scrum – when some say the atmosphere is even more lively. They open up the patio for barbecues in hot weather.

Main food type: Scottish/French
Licensed: Yes
Tables: Smoking 25; Non–smoking 0
Approximate cost: £6 – £12
Cards: All major cards
Open: 7 days 08.00–24.00
Disabled access: No

CAFE GANDOLFI
64 Albion Street, G1   552 6813

Gandolfi is probably the finest example of the Glasgow cafe-bar genre and has retained a loyal following despite the nearby City Halls having been downgraded in importance with the opening of a new concert hall.

It's the kind of place you can feel comfortable in at any time of the day. A late breakfast or supremely good morning coffee and croissants are Gandolfi's strong points. Lunch can be expensive – there are ambitious and changing blackboard specials – but you can hold costs down by opting for cheaper snacks, salads or cakes.

In the evening, the ambience is more sophisticated with candlelit tables and earnest young couples. Recommended dishes include choux pastry stuffed with stilton and marinated herring and potato salad. The atmosphere is rather special and difficult to define. Popular with business people, lawyers, students, theatre goers – this is one of the few places people are prepared to queue patiently for. Look out for the stained glass fishes as well as Tim Stead's furniture.

Main food style: Scottish
Licensed: Yes
Tables: Smoking 17; Non–smoking 0
Approximate cost: £10 – £15
Cards: None
Open: M–Sat 09.00–23.30;
        Sun 09.00–17.00 (for light snacks)
Disabled access: Yes

CANTINETTA QUI
Italian Centre, John Street, G1   552 6099

The ground floor cafe shares space with rivals which is all very confusing. An attractive spot to sit and sip your cappuccino while gazing at passers-by gazing at you gazing at them, Sicilian-style. Here you pay for atmosphere and a brief escape from grey Scottish reality. Descend into the Cantinetta dungeon and find yourself in a strange world of expressionist murals and (plastic?) plants. The lighting is dim.

The menu is compact but impressively breaks out of the usual pasta/pizza cliches: grilled mussels in a green sauce; crab, prawn and saffron chowder; monkfish with cream and rice; grilled salmon filled with honey, cinnamon, zest of orange. Most of the chef's ambitions are more than adequately realised, though the rich sauces and exotic flavourings may prove too challenging for some. Desserts are more familiar and rewarding if you have avoided the temptation to over-indulge at the main course.

Main food style: Italian
Licensed: Yes
Tables: Smoking 50; Non–smoking 0
Approximate cost: £6 – £25
Cards: All cards except Switch
Open: M–Sat 10.00–24.00; Sun 11.00–23.30
Disabled access: Cafe Yes; Restaurant No

The CITY MERCHANT
97 Candleriggs, G1   553 1577

The City Merchant has been steadily building a strong
reputation over the years. The loss of most of the
symphony concerts from the City Halls across the
street appeared to inflict little damage on its fortunes.
On the contrary, it has expanded into the cellar as
The City Basement bar-cafe.

The main restaurant is pleasant enough but far from
spacious. The menu features an impressive variety of
dishes, but with an emphasis on fish and steak. There
are also pastas and vegetarian choices. This is
formidable cooking, displayed to its full effect in
Zuppa di Pesce (£3.95 as a starter or £7.95 as a main
course), fillet steak with oysters and cajun butter
(£13.95) and grilled fillet of turbot with pink
peppercorn and julienne of vegetables (£9.95).
There's an ambitious Taste of Scotland menu to
delight foreign guests: cullen skink (£3.50), roast
pheasant with wild mushroom and red wine (£9.95)
and the Scottish cheeseboard with oatcakes (£3.75).
The sweets in general are exceptional. The wine list
has been knowledgably constructed. To complete a
memorable evening, you can drink cappuccino,
espresso, standard or decaffeinated coffee, or Scottish
blend, Earl Grey, rosehip, peppermint or camomile
tea served with petits fours. Highly recommended.

Main food style: Scottish/International
Licensed: Yes
Tables: Smoking 15; Non–smoking 0
Approximate cost: £8 – £25
Cards: All major cards
Open: M–Sat 12.00–14.30, 17.30–23.00; Sun closed
Disabled access: Yes

FIRE STATION
33 Ingram Street, G1   552 2929

The Merchant City specialises in the transformation of
buildings constructed for one purpose into something
utterly unconnected. The distinctive feature of the
Fire Station is how similar it looks and feels to a fire
station. Take out the fire engines, shove in some
tables and chairs and – voila! An exaggeration, of
course, but the sensation of being in a cavernous
garage which is merely masquerading as a restaurant
is a strong one.

Having said that, children find the idea entertaining
and the less than sympathetic dimensions are no
obstacle to passing an enjoyable hour or two
munching burgers, pastas or salads in the company
of an enthusiastic if slightly anarchic staff. The menu
descriptions are genuinely witty. Good for
vegetarians, less so for wine buffs. Desserts are large,
sticky and sweet – in other words, worth killing for.
Particularly cheap early on weekday evenings. Live
music or cabaret would go down a treat here.

Main food style: International
Licensed: Yes
Tables: Smoking 14; Non–smoking 14
Approximate cost: £5 – £12
Cards: Access; Switch; Visa
Open: 7 days 12.30–14.30, 17.00–23.00
Disabled access: Yes

INDITA
6 John Street, G1   553 1950

First the bad news. Indita was originally Indo-Italian (always an unlikely mix) but has ditched the Indian connection in favour of Spain, resulting in a bit of an identity crisis. The good news is that the prognosis looks healthy.

The menu makes more gastronomic sense and prices have fallen. Located just opposite the Italian Centre, the physical attributes of the dining room are glorious. You descend into a cool and elegant world of marble and mirrors, already convinced that this is a high-class joint before you've tasted a mouthful. The impressive decor is matched by polished and attentive waitering.

It would be difficult for the food to live up to the setting, but it's highly acceptable all the same. Fish and pastas are probably the strong points, and the accompaniments are fresh and plentiful. The staff coped brilliantly with a complaint about a piece of marginally undercooked sole. A plea to the chef: build up the Spanish dimension – there's plenty spaghetti across the street.

Main food style: Spanish/Italian
Licensed: Yes
Tables: Smoking 12; Non–smoking 0
Approximate cost: £7 – £17
Cards: All major cards
Open: M–Sat 12.00–14.30, 17.30–22.45; Sun closed
Disabled access: No

INN on the GREEN
23 Greenhead Street, G40   554 0165

Live music and clubby atmosphere draw the crowds
at week-ends, but the ivories also tinkle during
quieter mid-week evenings. The £6.50 pre-theatre
menu (2 courses and coffee) has a couple of
vegetarian choices and is excellent value but last
orders for these are at the early hour of 7pm.

Starters overlap in price (£2 – £6) with main courses
(£6 – £13), but the single portion of crudities was
enough for two. The chicken tasted wonderful in its
whiskey and mustard sauce, but there just wasn't
enough of the poor creature to satisfy a healthy adult
appetite. Vege-lasagne was delicious and similarly
rationed. Fortunately, a plentiful supply of vegetables
(plain but expertly cooked) saved the day.

Desserts all sound tempting – apple strudel and ice
cream turned out to be a rewarding choice. The
carafe of house white wine was decently chilled but
at the sweeter end of "medium dry". Strong freshly
ground coffee (no mints or refills) rounded off a
basically pleasurable evening. If you lose interest in
the food you can sit back and enjoy the piano
playing or scan the pictures on the walls. Look out
for the colourful stained glass.

Main food style: International
Licensed: Yes
Tables: Smoking 23; Non–smoking 2
Approximate cost: £7 – £20
Cards: Access; AmEx; Visa
Open: M–F 12.00–15.00; T–Sat 17.00–'till late;
         Sun by arrangement
Disabled access: No

St. MUNGO MUSEUM Cafeteria
2 Cathedral Street G4   553 2598

The original idea was a sensible one: to serve food that would be acceptable to all the major religions featured in the museum. Why on earth spoil it with the gratuitous inclusion of braised steak (£3.25)? Why not offer examples of food associated with different religious traditions? Why is such a brilliant concept for a new museum so indifferently executed? There are no obvious answers to these questions, nor any evidence that the organisers would even understand them.

On the other hand, the building is a better one than its critics would have us believe and could eventually be used more effectively. The (self-service) cafe is clean and welcoming and is already attracting both tourists and docs (attached to bleeps) from the Royal Infirmary. Vegetable soup was thick and richly flavoured. Soup is always vegetarian and there is one vegetarian and one meat dish every day. The limited selection of sandwiches, salads and cakes were fresh and healthy looking. Because of the location there should be no shortage of custom.

Main food style: British
Licensed: Yes
Tables: Smoking 0; Non–smoking 12
Approximate cost: £4 – £6
Cards: None
Open: M–Sat 10.00–16.30; Sun 11.00–16.30
Disabled access: Yes

PASSTICCERIA FRANCOIS
Italian Centre, Cochrane St., G1   552 7330

The pavement cafes of the Italian Centre only come into their own on the three days in the year when the sun shines. The rest of the time the area looks forlorn and neglected, like a film set abandoned in mid-shoot due to money problems.

The Passticceria Francois, as its name suggests, is drawn back to its French roots despite pretending to be Italian. The results include Insalata Nicoise (£3.85), filled croissants (around £3) and profiteroles (£1.95). Soups, pastas and desserts are all worth sampling. The menu descriptions wax lyrical: the Stregat (£2.20) is described as "layers of Strega liqueur soaked sponge filled with almond flavoured cream topped with Amaretto biscuits and melted chocolate". How could you refuse?

One small cavil: the waitresses had a dreamy, distracted quality, as if they'd just met George Michael. Our trivial concerns, like crumbs on the table or a request for the bill, could have been a million miles away.

Main food style: Italian
Licensed: Yes
Tables: Smoking 23; Non–smoking 0
Approximate cost: £5 – £14
Cards: Access; Delta; Eurocard; Mastercard; Visa
Open: M–Sat 08.00–19.00; Sun 11.00–17.00
Disabled access: Yes

RAB HA's
83 Hutcheson Street, G1   553 1545

Happily back in business after a period of closure, this old Scots hostelry is exactly the kind of facility the Merchant City needs to pull in visitors. Unless you are unfortunate enough to arrive unexpectedly on a weekend evening when the tiny building looks set to explode with revellers, both the ground floor pub and the basement restaurant will provide unalloyed pleasure.

The menu refuses to conform to the stereotypically Scottish (no bad thing) but perhaps misses an opportunity to stamp an ethnic identity on the cooking. Courgette and cauliflower soup was exquisite, served with plentiful fresh bread. Other starters are port and stilton pate, saute mushroom in creamy garlic sauce, mussels with coriander and pink peppercorns. Memorable main courses include vegetarian stroganoff (with a delicately flavoured sauce that few kitchens could match), and char-grilled sirloin steak.

Desserts feature several successful creations: apricot and orange mousse, plum and apple crumble are two. The pre-theatre prices are around £7 (two courses) and £9 (three courses). Service is delightful, a fine advertisement for local hospitality.

Main food style: British/European
Licensed: Yes
Tables: Smoking 19; Non–smoking 0
Approximate cost: £8 – £20
Cards: All major cards
Open: 7 days 11.00–24.00
Disabled access: No

TRON THEATRE CAFE-BAR
Trongate, G1   552 8587

The Tron goes from strength to strength, and its
continuing theatrical success attracts ever more
participants to its less artistic activities – specifically
the consumption of quality food and drink. A steady
managerial hand is everywhere evident.

The menu has continental leanings with abundant
vegetarian possibilities. Soup is seldom less than
glorious. Many of the dishes are available as either
starters or main courses and the staff are flexible
about content. Fish is always a shrewd choice:
salmon cakes are the desired taste, texture and
consistency. Garnishings are colourful and nutritious.

The main drawback is physical – the intimate mixing
of diners and drinkers may be highly sociable
(particularly as audience and actors collide after a
performance) but it can work against the pleasure of
dining. The adjoining coffee bar extension is
altogether more peaceful and now provides self-
service snacks (including baked potatoes, cauliflower
and cheese, salads and pies) if you prefer to avoid
the crush of the main bar.

Main food style: International
Licensed: Yes
Tables: Smoking 11; Non–smoking 9
Approximate cost: £5 – £12
Cards: Mastercard; Visa
Open: M–T 12.00–15.00, 17.00–23.00;
     F&Sat 12.00–23.00;
     Sun 10.30–16.00, 17.00–22.00
Disabled access: Yes

WAREHOUSE
61-65 Glassford Street, G1   552 4181

A local wit is reported to have directed a thirsty
tourist into the Warehouse with the comment: "Ye
canny miss it – it's where all the dummies are
standin' aboot". Whether or not this was intended as
an insult to the clientele of this fashionable clothes
shop we shall probably never know. From your
strategic position at the ground floor sandwich bar,
you will have Armani, Gaultier and the other
designer labels in your sights.

Take the lift to third floor where you can join the fray
in a lively cafe serving a fair range of lightish snacks
such as quiches, baked potatoes, filled croissants and
cakes. Some of these are substantial although the
price may cause you pause for thought: salade
nicoise (£3.95), smoked salmon and cream cheese on
a bagel, hot pastrami on rye (both £4.50). Of the few
wines available, Muscadet at £6.50 a bottle looks a
good buy. There are five varieties of tea. The staff are
well-trained and chirpy. Seats have to be fought over
at peak times.

Main food style: International
Licensed: Yes
Tables: Smoking 15; Non–smoking 0
Approximate cost: £6 – £8
Cards: All cards
Open: M–Sat 10.00–18.00; Sun closed
Disabled access: Yes, in elevator

XO (Cathedral House)

28-32 Cathedral Square, G4   552 3519

There are two reasons why this new enterprise might
flourish. First, this is a fast-developing tourist area
which has not yet woken up to the needs of hungry
visitors. And second, how many people have heard
of – let alone tried – Icelandic cooking? Moreover,
the physical attractions of the dining room are
unrivalled. The view of the cathedral precinct,
particularly as the sun sets and the floodlighting is
switched on, is spectacular. The interior design is
inspired, with clever partitioning providing a feeling
of privacy in most parts of the dining area.

The verdict on the food must be more cautious.
Onion soup was magnificent. Fish and game
speciality main courses were competently prepared
and vegetables were tasty if not overly thrilling. The
novelties are the hot rock dishes which you can cook
yourself at your table – not recommended on a warm
evening. A snag – quantities of meat and fish were
sparse. At these prices, this could be a fatal flaw.

Main food style: Icelandic/European
Licensed: Yes
Tables: Smoking 12; Non-smoking 0
Approximate cost: £15 – £25
Cards: Access; AmEx; Diners; Visa
Open: M–Sat 18.30–22.30; Sun closed
Disabled access: No

THE SOUTH SIDE

The South Side is the site of the once notorious (and now largely demolished) Gorbals, the Citizens' and Tramway theatres, the Victorian garden suburb of Pollokshields and the magnificent Burrell Collection. Beyond the lively shopping centre of Shawlands lies a great swathe of parklands (including the famous beauty spot of Rouken Glen), golf courses and extensive residential suburbs.

ATHENA
778 Pollokshaws Road, G41   424 0858

This tiny room, described as a Greek Taverna, has an adjoining bar which often looks empty. The Athena cannot compete with The Parthenon or Serghei in sophistication, but the cooking is closer to the real thing.

Portions are large, the food is tasty. If you are none too keen on Greek food, don't come, because few compromises are made to satisfy the British palate. Bean soup is magnificent, served in a huge vat with plenty of fresh bread. Vegetable moussaka will be too heavily spiced for some. Olive oil is used liberally. Desserts are rather variable.

The staff are anxious to please. Because of the small space, conversation is inhibited – as is breathing when ciggies are lit. This is the kind of place to come if you are tired of glitz and gloss. Here you get back to basics – and you'll be none the worse for that.

Main food style: Greek
Licensed: Yes
Tables: Smoking 14; Non–smoking 0
Approximate cost: £5 – £14
Cards: None
Open: M–Sat 12.00–14.30, 17.00–23.00; Sun closed
Disabled access: Yes

CAFE BLANKITT
378 Cathcart Road, G42　　　　423 5172

Associated with Philip Raskin, who confounded the
sceptics by opening The Inn on the Green in
Bridgeton, the Cafe Blankitt is another example of
courageous business thinking. "Hampstead in
Govanhill" is the ironic sub-title of this pretty cafe-
bistro located within an unusual gift shop. The
surrounding area has nowhere else appealing. The
result – the place is jam-packed at lunchtime.
Because the room is so small, smokers can
thoroughly spoil your enjoyment. As well as the
usual cafe snacks, there are interesting items: bagels
and smoked salmon, quail pate and salad (£3.60).
The soft drink selection contains the odd surprise too
– what on earth is Israeli Spring Nectar?

Eventually, new housing and shopping developments
may revitalise this forgotten part of Glasgow. Until
that happens, we should be grateful for small mercies
– like Cafe Blankitt – to demonstrate what can be
achieved.

Main food style: International
Licensed: Yes
Tables: Smoking 8; Non–smoking 6
Approximate cost: £5 – £8
Cards: All major cards
Open: M–T 08.30–17.30;
　　　F&Sat 08.30–16.30, 19.00–'til late;
　　　Sun 10.30–16.30
Disabled access: Yes

CAFE SERGHEI
67 Bridge Street, G5   429 1547

The Eastern Mediterranean has made minimal impact
on the Glasgow restaurant scene. The handful of
serious Greek chefs working in the city appear to
make a good living and it is curious that there are not
more. Cafe Serghei represents an enormous
investment in an old commercial building near the
riverside, and must be regarded as something of a
gamble given its awkward accessibility (although its
proximity to the Citizens' Theatre may prove
advantageous). The interior is a remarkable
achievement, with some original artefacts preserved
intact and others adapted to new purposes. The best
view of the high ceilinged room is from the balcony
at the top of the spiral staircase. The solid wooden
furniture is comfortable as well as aesthetic.

The menu is varied and lends itself to the selection of
several side dishes for group sharing. The cooking is
highly competent, neither too spicy nor oily, and
garnishing is pleasing with fresh salads and
vegetables. The three course business lunch is easily
the best value (£5.50), but there is also a pre-theatre
menu (£7.50) which comes a close second. Every
now and again, the waiters insist on performing
energetic Greek dancing.

Main food style: Greek/European
Licensed: Yes
Tables: 33; Smoking/Non-smoking segregation is
        arranged
Approximate cost: £5.50 – £17
Cards: Access; Visa
Open: M–S 12.—14.30, 17.00–23.00 (last orders):
        Sun 18.00–23.00
Disabled access: Yes

The CHERRY TREE
55 Eastwoodmains Road, G46   620 3315

Mention the name Williamwood, an unremarkable
suburb nestling between Giffnock and Clarkston, and
the image of bohemian cafe society is unlikely to
spring to mind. The Cherry Tree fills a gaping chasm
which is greatly appreciated by locals (visitors, other
than travellers to somewhere else who have lost their
way, being virtually unheard of here).

There is nothing exceptional about this unpretentious
corner cafe (except, perhaps, for the fact of its
existence), but it is a friendly little place offering
sandwiches, baked potatoes and good home baking.
Hot drinks are reliable. All age groups are welcome
and young children particularly seem to take delight
in its story-book quaintness. Prices are fair. A cause
worthy of support, not least "pour encourager les
autres" as they say in these parts.

Main food style: British
Licensed: No
Tables: Smoking 8; Non-smoking 0
Approximate cost: £3 – £7
Cards: None
Open: M-S 10.00–16.30; Sun closed
Disabled access: Yes

The CHURCH on the HILL
16 Algie Street, G42   649 5189

The imposing neo-classical facade of this fine old
church facing the Langside Monument was always
one of the architectural highlights of this part of the
city. For too long it lay in a semiderelict state and
seemed destined for the bulldozer. Now it has been
saved for posterity by the present owners.

The diner-style menu is fairly pedestrian – fried
mushrooms, potato skins in the starter section,
chicken Maryland, steak pie, burgers among the main
courses. On the other hand, the food is better than it
sounds. Soup is freshly made daily (you can tell by
the flavour) and is served with baguette and butter
(£1.45). Haddock and chips, garnished, is under a
fiver. Steaks are cooked blue (almost raw), rare,
medium or well done (around £9). There are several
vegetarian possibilities (including a tasty Chinese stir
fry). The wine list is short but includes half-litres.
Desserts look mouth-watering (mostly under £2).

Staff are friendly and are unfazed by children. The
building looks at its magnificent best after dark under
floodlighting .

Main food style: International/American
Licensed: Yes
Tables: Smoking 15 (no cigars or pipes);
        Non-smoking 0
Approximate cost: £7 – £20
Cards: Access; Switch; Visa
Open: M–T 12.00–14.30, 17.00–22.30;
        F&Sat 12.00–23.00; Sun 12.30–22.30
Disabled access: Yes

DOLOMITI

164 Darnley Street, G41   423 6694

Why this area is so ill-stocked with restaurants is a mystery. The Tramway Theatre is within shouting distance and there's fast transport into town. Dolomiti has the field to itself but, ominously, is the third occupant of the site in as many years. Nevertheless, this compact Italian trattoria will fight hard and may triumph for it has already established an embryonic reputation and a local following.

The menu is predictable but the food is fresh, competently cooked and professionally presented. Starters are expensive (this is a worrying city-wide trend) – skip these unless you are ravenous. The soup is first-rate. Substantial fish and meat courses are complemented by side dishes of vegetables immaculately cooked. Pastas a-plenty – and they'll at least match expectations. Coffee was an anticlimax – refills were accordingly declined. The solo waiter was fascinating to watch: an extra pair of hands would have diminished the entertainment but improved the service.

Main food style: Italian
Licensed: Yes
Tables: Smoking 8; Non-smoking 0
Approximate cost: £10 – £25
Cards: All major cards
Open: M–S 12.00–14.30, 18.00–23.00; Sun closed
Disabled access: Yes but small toilet

DUCA Di PARMA
480 Paisley Road, G5   420 3003

Some claim that this recently opened little ristorante
is rapidly overtaking the nearby La Fiorentina in
nearly every department. Although tiny, its ambitions
are high. Don't rush your meal – or the chef – since
everything emerging from the kitchen deserves to be
appreciated at leisure.

Minestrone is classic, the pastas are superlative and
the well chosen cuts of steak, veal and fish are
cooked with devotion. Vegetables are treated with
respect and provided generously. Desserts and coffee
maintain the excellent standard. The wine list is more
than adequate. Service is considerate and helpful. In
short, one has to enthuse about virtually every aspect
of the meal, from the selection of the original
ingredients to the presentation of the finished
product.

The location is less than ideal, perhaps, although
lovers of good Italian food will not be deterred.
Budget price meals (lunch, pre-theatre) are bound to
be popular. Because of its size, privacy may be
difficult to preserve when a hungry mob arrives. Must
be a contender for the most promising new Italian
restaurant in the city.

Main food style: Italian
Licensed: Yes
Tables: Smoking 10; Non-smoking 0 but non-smokers
**   catered for**
Approximate cost: £6 – £20
Cards: All major cards
Open: M–F 12.00–14.00, 17.30–22.45; S 17.30–22.45 &
**   (if 'Gers at home 12.00–14.00); Sun closed**
Disabled access: Yes

La FIORENTINA
2 Paisley Road West, G51   420 1585

Question: which famous European building inspired
the architect of the tenement housing La Fiorentina?
(Answers on a postcard please). Govan is no longer
totally ignored by the restaurant trade, merely
unjustly neglected.

This spacious and comfortable Ristorante Trattoria
(can it be both?) is the pioneer and draws its custom
from a wide area. The menu now bears an uncanny
resemblance to La Riviera in Partick – for which there
may be sound managerial reasons. The food is nearly
always excellent and the helpings generous. Fresh
vegetables are copious. The wine list offers ample
opportunity to deviate from the house white which
can be too sweet for some. The three course lunch or
pre-theatre menu at £5.95 represents a bargain. Staff
are polite and helpful. Parking across the road is
semi-supervised.

Main food style: Italian
Licensed: Yes
Tables: Smoking 29; Non-smoking 0 but segregation
         on lower level
Approximate cost: £6 – £20
Cards: All major cards
Open: M–S 12.00–14.30, 17.30–22.30; Sun closed
Disabled access: Yes

FREED's
49 Coplaw Street, G42   423 8911

One of the best kept secrets in town, Freed's seems
determined not to expand its small clientele. You
don't have to be Jewish to adore these cholesterol-
laden East European treats – from chopped liver to
lokshen pudding. Delicacies such as helzel and
tsimes may be unfamiliar to Scottish palates, but then
so were poppadoms and chow mein at one time.
There are fish alternatives and plenty of vegetables
for those preferring to avoid meat.

If you're feeling a shade under the weather on one of
those freezing, windswept days of which there are
about 300 a year in Glasgow, order chicken soup and
you'll understand why it's known as Jewish penicillin.
Busy on Sunday lunchtimes but otherwise you can
usually get a table. Apart from the ethnic menu, there
is a sad lack of atmosphere. The room needs radical
redesigning, preferably in more accessible premises.
Blooms of Whitechapel must have started out like
this and now has a world-wide reputation.

Main food style: Continental/ Kosher
Licensed: No (but bring own Kosher drinks)
Tables: Smoking 11; Non–smoking 0
Approximate cost: £5 – £10
Cards: None
Open: Sun–T 12.30–14.30, 17.30–20.00; F&Sat closed
Disabled access: Yes (with prior knowledge)

The GRANARY
10 Kilmarnock Road, G41   632 8487

The noise on a busy evening (and most are) can be overwhelming. This is because the restaurant is really an appendage of the pub, one of the most famous on the South Side and full of extraordinary artefacts. A great spot for people-watching, the food here seems of secondary importance to the many customers intent on socialising.

There must have been a shake-up in the kitchen in recent years, for the standard of cooking has risen strikingly. Leek and mushroom soup, or potato skins are both memorable starters. For a main course, try the exceptional honey-glazed lamb kebabs with rice. The Mexican dishes are seriously spicy – and said to score highly on authenticity. Portions range from large to massive.

The hard-working staff cope admirably under pressure, but a rethink of the seating plan would make their life easier and the diners more comfortable. The flowers on the tables were slightly dead, but the thought was nice. Definitely not for those seeking an oasis of tranquillity.

Main food style: Mexican/International
Licensed: Yes
Tables: Smoking 12; Non–smoking 0
Approximate cost: £10 –£25
Cards: All cards
Open: M–T 11.00–23.00; F–Sat 11.00–'till late;
    Sun 12.30–14.30, 18.00–24.00
Disabled access: Yes

Di MAGGIO's
1038 Pollokshaws Road, G41   632 4194

Shawlands draws enormous crowds of shoppers,
especially at weekends, and is the sort of area in
which you would expect to find lots of good
restaurants. Sadly, this is not the case – entrepreneurs
please note. Fortunately, there are bright spots – one
of them thanks to the Di Maggio empire.

This branch is charmed – reports of negative
experiences are as rare as canaries in Lapland. As you
enter, you have the sensation of stepping into a
transplanted corner of Italy. Choose a table by the
window: the one-way glass allows you to peer out
unobserved at the endless procession of Shawlands
pedestrians most of whom look as though a spirit-
lifting nosh-up would do them a world of good. The
most riveting action, however, takes place inside this
permanently packed pizzeria.

The food is consistently agreeable: garlic bread to
accompany minestrone never fails, the pizzas are
unrivalled and the pastas delightful. Not the perfect
spot for that quiet romantic dinner for two, yet diners
are reluctant to leave in case they miss anything
exciting. One of the most endearing features of the
staff is the genuine welcome they extend to families
with young children.

Main food style: Italian
Licensed: Yes
Tables: Smoking 26; Non-smoking 0
Approximate cost: £5 – £15
Cards: Access; AmEx; Switch; Visa
Open: M–F 12.00–14.30; M–T 17.00–24.00;
      F 17.00–01.00; S 12.00–01.00; Sun 17.00–24.00
Disabled access: Yes

MOYRA JANE's
20 Kildrostan Street, G41   423 5628

This is a potentially charming corner of Pollokshields all but ruined by the lunatic placement of bins and bottle banks on what should have been a pretty grass verge in the centre of the square. Fortunately, the area should recover, particularly if enterprises of the imagination and quality of Moyra Jane's set up shop. Housed in a former bank, this is one of the most attractive and welcoming coffee shops in the South Side. The room is spacious and tastefully decorated with bookshelves, prints and other quirky features. The furniture is solid and comfortable.

The menu is also a welcome departure from the norm: duck and port pate, toasties with wonderful fillings (smoked salmon, turkey and cranberry sauce, mortadella and mustard, cheese with peach chutney). But don't miss out on the soup. The coffee is fresh and strong. Prices are fair. The windows could do with screening or curtains but that may come. Word is spreading fast that Moyra's is no ordinary cafe – you may not get a table at lunchtime. A brilliant new arrival which sets a standard for others to beat.

Main food style: European
Licensed: No
Tables: Smoking 5; Non–smoking 6
Approximate cost: £4.50 – £8
Cards: Access; Visa; Mastercard
Open: M–F 09.00–17.00; Sat 09.00–16.30; Sun closed
Disabled access: Yes, but no disabled toilets

PARKLANDS COUNTRY CLUB
Crookfur Park, Ayr Road, G77   639 9222

Prior to the opening of this multi-purpose sports and
leisure centre, local worthies were up in arms at the
prospect of their sleepy suburban lives being
disturbed by such an alien intrusion. Now the place
is bursting at the seams with swimmers, squash
players and aerobic dancers most of whom appear to
come from the immediate neighbourhood.

One of the attractions is undoubtedly the comfortable
bar and restaurant complex which is open to non-
members. The relatively informal coffee shop has
large round tables overlooking the park, and the
enormous picture windows are opened in the
summer for ventilation. This is a popular spot for
families since it serves a range of snacks and light
meals including soups, salads, various vegetarian
concoctions and rattling good fish and chips.

The more up-market La Bonne Auberge has a
reputation for competent French-style cuisine at
highish prices. The kitchen staff can turn their hands
to other international forms of cooking which they
display to impressive effect on regular speciality
"ethnic" evenings. It is not unusual to arrive mid-
evening to find an hour-long queue for a table.

Main food style: International
Licensed: Yes
Tables: Smoking 37; Non-smoking 8
Approximate cost: £8 – £23
Cards: All except Switch
Open: M–S 12.00–14.30, 18.00–22.00;
         Sun 12.00–15.00, 17.30–21.00
Disabled access: Yes

PIAF's
87 Kilmarnock Road, G41   649 3141

The name is inspired, but any French connection is otherwise pretty tenuous. By day, Piaf's could be described as a sort of Glaswegian brasserie; by night, it reverts to a noisy pub like hundreds of others, complete with bouncers. From the outside, it looks deceptively small but there is a recessed rear room which is well ventilated even when busy. There are arty photographs on the walls and the seating is comfortable.

Lunchtime is madly busy, as if the food were free (it isn't). The menu has fairly standard cafe offerings – baked potatoes, croissants, cakes. Portions are substantial and everything tastes fresh. The cappuccinos are famed for their size and quality. Prices are reasonable. The sort of place a couple of friends are wont to sit for an hour or two over a glass of Burgundy tearing other mutual friends, acquaintances and family members to tiny shreds in relative safety and privacy.

Piaf's may never reach Olympian heights, gastronomic or social, but it does seem to have found a niche somewhere in the lower foothills.

Main food style: British
Licensed: Yes
**Tables: Smoking 14; Non-smoking 0 but segregation
        possible**
Approximate cost: £6 – £8
Cards: All major cards
Open: M–S 10.30–20.00 (last orders); Sun 12.00–18.00
Disabled access: Yes

SCOOZI's
36 The Avenue, G77   616 0088

The Avenue is a large shopping mall which attracts droves of well-heeled suburbanites at weekends. This is a captive market for a restaurant and Scoozi's has begun to tap into it.

Described as a trattoria and deli-bar (where does one end and the other begin?), there are two contrasting customer types: distraught parents (usually fathers) seeking a diversion for disillusioned offspring, and teenagers indulging in ritualistic greetings of long-lost friends last encountered in school an hour earlier. Not a place to linger for a cordon bleu epic, the light snacks and daily specials are better than the average cafe of its type. Good ones to try are cauliflower and potato bake (£4.85) and lasagna (£3.65). Sunday brunch is available from 10 am. In the evening, you can have a more elaborate meal and some reports are encouraging – but menus are in the process of being revamped. Watch this space.

Main food style: Italian/International
Licensed: Yes
Tables: Smoking 30; Non-smoking 0
Approximate cost: £6 – £12
Cards: None
Open: 7 days 09.00–22.30 (last orders)
Disabled access: Yes

The SEPOY CLUB (Dalmeny Hotel)
62 St Andrews Drive, G41   427 1106/6288

The Sepoy Club is the South Side's answer to the Killermont Polo Club in the West End. You enter by the front door of the hotel, from where you are led through to the restaurant which is in two sections. Try to be seated in the conservatory which is a delight. There is a profusion of colour and vegetation which induce a lovely sensation of relaxation.

The menu is unusual, employing numerous variants of the standard curries, biryanis and kormas. Service is extremely amiable and highly efficient. The wine list is comprehensive. Just sit back and let them bring dish after dish of the most interestingly cooked and delicately spiced Indian food you will find anywhere.

The rare slip-up is handled with tact and professionalism. Perhaps not yet quite in the Killermont class, but heading in that direction slowly and steadily. If it can maintain the momentum, the plaudits will start rolling in.

Main food style: Indian
Licensed: Yes
Tables: Smoking 19; Non–smoking 0
Approximate cost: £8 – £15
Cards: All major cards
Open: M–F 12.00–14.00; M–Sun 17.00–22.30
Disabled access: Yes

TURBAN
2 Station Road, G46   638 0069

Competition in the Asian food sector is now so
intense in Glasgow that only the elite are likely to
flourish. This long-established tandoori restaurant,
handily located next to Giffnock station car park, has
won both brickbats and plaudits in the past but is
currently in superlative form. Lighting is tastefully
subdued, taped music is not too loud, ventilation is
good and the service is highly professional and good-
humoured. Cubicalised seating is comfortable and, in
places, conveys a feeling of total privacy.

The menu is relatively short, but that is no great
disadvantage. One portion of pakora sufficed for two
and had that perfect combination of a crisp outer
coating with a soft-textured centre. Saffron rice was
delectable, ideally complementing chicken patia with
its subtle hint of sweet and sour flavouring. Chapatis
and parathas could not conceivably have been
bettered. Hot towels are distributed to help you mop
up the sauces from your beard. For those who can
taste it through the spices, the wine list is attractive:
Indian champagne sounds intriguing. If you ask for
water, you get a large jug with plenty of ice rather
than the usual miserable tumblerful. Overall, an
outstandingly pleasurable experience. Maintaining
this high standard will not be easy. Highly
recommended.

Main food style: Indian
Licensed: Yes
Tables: 19, Smoking segregated by request
Approximate cost: £8 – £15
Cards: All major cards except Diners and Switch
Open: 7 days 17.00–24.00
Disabled access: Yes, but restricted toilet access

La VECCHIA ROMAGNA
108 Ayr Road, G77   639 1162

Given that Eastwood is arguably the most prosperous
suburb in Scotland, it is extraordinarily thin on
passable eating places. La Vecchia almost has the
field to itself if you want a no-nonsense, no-frills
family meal at a moderate cost. Before 7pm, three
courses will cost under £8 – thereafter the more
extensive and expensive (£12.50) table d'hote
appears.

They do minestrone with their eyes shut, but ask
about the soup of the day: carrot and basil was a
revelation. Fresh white bread was offered (once). Egg
mornay was counted a success if not a masterpiece
of culinary art. Sole caprice could scarcely have been
bettered though the accompanying new potatoes
were lukewarm. Pastas and seafood have been
mentioned favourably in dispatches. Portions were
modest.

Of the extensive dessert menu, Italian fudge cake
won plaudits. Coffee is good'n strong. The overall
level of comfort needs attention: the chair backs are
unfriendly to the human spine and the seating plan is
awkward: unless you choose your spot carefully,
privacy is zero. Lovely Italian taped music.

Main food style: Italian
Licensed: Yes
Tables: Smoking 16; Non–smoking 0
Approximate cost: £8 – £25
Cards: Access; AmEx; Diners; Visa
Open: M–Sat 12.00–14.00, 17.30–22.00; Sun closed
Disabled access: Yes

WOK WAY
2 Burnfield Road, G46   638 2244

In some ways, publicity is the last thing this
minuscule restaurant needs, so limited is its
accommodation. What it lacks in scale it more than
compensates for in everything else – enthusiasm,
cooking skills and panache. Most of its trade revolves
around carry-outs and home deliveries, but the
experience of sitting in its delightful dining room is
one to savour.

The food is prepared in any of four styles: Peking,
Hunan, Szechuan or Cantonese. The staff will advise
on this but try the exquisite beef in Hunan style (it
comes with seasonal vegetables, hot bean sauce and
cashew nuts). Sweet and sour lemon sole is a rarity
and is usually excellent. The banana fritters are
adored by younger family members. None of this
need upset you bank manager, unless you go the
whole hog and have the Mandarin Feast (£25)
washed down by a bottle of Jouet (£65) – on second
thoughts, consider (if you dare) Great Wall of China
(white) at £10.

Main food style: Chinese
Licensed: Yes
Tables: Smoking 6; Non-smoking 0
Approximate cost: £8 – £25
Cards: All major cards
Open: Sun–W 17.00–24.00;
     T 12.00–14.00, 17.00–24.00;
     F 12.00–23.00; S 14.00–01.00
Disabled access: No

Index